THE
SPIRITUAL PATHWAY
TO
FREEDOM

Lectures on Christian Science

by

John H. Wyndham

and

Glen C. Livezey

Mountaintop Publishing

Photography: Michael G. Kelly

ISBN # 978-1-893930-04-9

MountaintopPublishing
California, U.S.A
www.MountaintopPublishing.com.

Table of Contents

INTRODUCTION

Just what is freedom? If you were to ask a few people, you would likely receive answers that point to freedom *from* some situation. For instance, many desire freedom from financial worry, from health problems, or from being tied down to a certain job. There is a yearning for higher good in our lives even if we don't know exactly what it is or how it might take shape.

Mary Baker Eddy wrote about that yearning in her main work, *Science and Health with Key to the Scriptures*: "The aspiration after heavenly good comes even before we discover what belongs to wisdom and Love."

Though we may not be able to envision exactly what true freedom is or what God, divine Love, has provided for us, that doesn't prevent us from desiring to leave behind the old for the yet-to-be known good that awaits us.

Even animals can have such a hope and rush towards it. A woman wrote a heart-warming piece about adopting a dog from a shelter in New York City, though she lived in just a small apartment there. She went to pick out the dog, had to wait a week for paperwork to be done, then went back to claim it.

The dog was so happy to see her again and, as they walked the twenty blocks to her apartment, that dog strained at the leash to go forward. The woman observed that the dog didn't know what it was *going to,* but knew what it was *coming from.*

Each lecture in this book shows the aspiration for heavenly good, and reveals how it was answered and by what means. The two men who gave these lectures, John Wyndham and Glen Livezey, could see what they were leaving, as clearly as one might see the shore recede from a ship departing a country, though they had yet to discover what was beyond their horizon. It is their journey and discovery in these lectures that will speak to your heart, and provide inspiration for your own life journey.

Who were these men and what of their times? They delivered their lectures to a wide range of audiences in many different countries during the 1960's and 1970's. As history shows that was a pivotal time for society at large, especially in the United States. It was a period in which civil rights, women's rights and a youthful rebellion took center stage. So tumultuous a time was it that a TV program with Tom Brokaw even suggested 1968 was the year that separated the past from the future. So what would John and Glen contribute?

These two men both served during World War II, though they were born twenty one years apart—one in a small town in Holland and the other in a small town in Ohio. They never met until decades later when their mission to help mankind brought them together. Interestingly, it was the discovery made by a woman which united them in this mission. At one point in the 1960's, John Wyndham sadly commented to me about the status of women. He said, "A woman is always some man's daughter, or some man's wife." He had learned through his own hard life experiences what valuable contributions women make to the advancement of mankind.

Glen Livezey also learned that fact through a life-changing event, though he had previously termed himself a "male chauvinist."

Now, I must say, that it is with great joy, love and an appreciation for the contributions these men made, that I publish this book of lectures—as the daughter of John and the wife of Glen.

The photographs on the cover and in this book were taken by Michael G. Kelly, an amateur photographer, during his treks across the Grand Canyon. Rather than the sweeping views one usually sees of the Canyon, these photos provide a more intimate view of the landscape.

What more fitting metaphor and introduction could we have for these lectures because, in fact, we are all just amateurs on this grand adventure, that of taking the spiritual pathway to freedom.

Auriel Wyndham Livezey

INTRODUCING JOHN H. WYNDHAM

As a young boy, growing up in Holland, John Wyndham could hear the sound of guns—the guns of World War I—in neighboring countries. As a young man, he left Holland for the United States, where he "heard" the sound of freedom, in the form of a book, which showed him how true freedom for himself and the whole world could be gained, not through guns but through a spiritual pathway. A few years later, he traveled again, this time from San Francisco to Sydney, Australia.

After World War II began, he enlisted in the Royal Australian Air Force, though by that time he was in his mid-30's with a wife and two small children. The advancing steps of John Wyndham's own spiritual journey can be seen most vividly in his prisoner-of-war experience in Java. His first lecture, "Do We Think or Just Think We Think?" explores the basic question he had to face when threatened with execution. What kind of thinking was he going to do and what part would it play in saving his life?

From this basis, it was not a far distance into a new dimension, a spiritual dimension for living, which could only be entered through right thinking and doing. His film-making in Africa, of which he speaks in his second lecture, "What are Your Dimensions for Living?" took place in the 1950's, when he was Director for Public Information for UNICEF, based first in New York and then in Paris.

INTRODUCTION

The spiritual dimension and the results of living in it are discussed throughout this lecture. A more complete chronology and description of that time in his life is found in his book, *The Ultimate Freedom.*

The third lecture, "The Divine Adventure" is a natural outcome of living in the spiritual dimension. However, these are not abstract or thought-only adventures, but are outwardly seen in our human experience. After serving with UNICEF, John lived in London then California, becoming a Christian Science practitioner, teacher, and a member of the Christian Science Board of Lectureship.

John Wyndham had longed to be a sea captain as he was growing up. And roam the seas he did, but usually by air, as he lectured worldwide in four languages, from 1968 to 1978. He spoke in English, Dutch, German and Afrikaans. From African villages to Carnegie Hall, his lectures were warmly welcomed. One audience of over five thousand people broke into spontaneous applause when he proclaimed,"There are three things God will not let you have. They are sin, sickness and death. All the rest you can have!"

These lectures are still well remembered for they provide practical answers to the issues we face in today's world. They help show that the spiritual pathway to freedom is truly the only way to go.

A.W.L.

DO WE THINK, OR JUST THINK WE THINK?

Do We Think or Just Think We Think?

John H. Wyndham, C.S.B.

During a conversation with a college student, I was struck by his oft-repeated statement, "I think." He repeated "I think" so many times that I finally asked him, "What do you mean by 'I think'? What do you consider thinking to be?" After some moments he admitted he was stumped.

The point is: "Do we think, or just think we think?" This question isn't intended as a catalyst to make us sit in judgment on ourselves or on one another. It's meant rather as a lie-detector, or better still as a truth-detector. Surely everyone here will agree that we all seek to know the truth about things. As this is so, we're also interested to know if our *thinking* is true. I hope that by exploring this subject together we shall come to know ourselves a little better and find out if we engage in that true thinking so important for worthwhile living.

Today the notion of thinking pervades our society. Research organizations are sometimes referred to as "think factories." In our daily life, we're constantly urged to think in some particular manner. Furnishing manufacturers plead "Think color." Beauty experts cry "Think young." Physical fitness promoters shout "Think thin."

More significant than this contemporary usage is the fact that men and women of great stature have earnestly considered the question of thinking. Perhaps we're all familiar with Shakespeare's statement, "There is nothing either good or bad, but thinking makes it so." In the Bible are these words attributed to Solomon, "As he [a man] thinketh in his heart, so is he" (Prov. 23:7). And Mary Baker Eddy, the Discoverer of Christian Science, in the Preface to her book, *Science and Health with Key to the Scriptures* has this rousing statement: "The time for thinkers has come" (p. vii).

Isn't it true that all of us are engaged in the business of thinking? But can we rightly say that what we call thinking is always true or original thinking? Isn't much of it reacting to impressions, or suggestions, or mulling over our problems and difficulties?

Many centuries ago the Roman philosopher Marcus Aurelius said: "The happiness of your life depends upon the quality of your thoughts, therefore guard them accordingly." This statement is just as true today as it was then, so the question of thinking is of vital importance to us all.

Through careful choice of the thoughts which come to us, we can do much to improve our whole life experience, as well as that of our neighbors. In order to experience good more fully, we need to differentiate clearly between real thinking and what is really not thinking at all. Then we need to control thought. That's to say we need to bar false thinking and keep busy with true thinking. Let me repeat the substance of this, for it's our main concern today. In order to experience good, we need to control our thought—bar false thinking, which isn't really thinking at all—and keep ourselves active with true thinking.

What Is True Thinking?

What constitutes true thinking? The Apostle Paul wrote: "Whatsoever things are true, whatsoever things are honest, whatsoever things are just, whatsoever things are pure, whatsoever things are lovely, whatsoever things are of good report; if there be any virtue, and if there be any praise, think on these things" (Phil. 4:8).

If to think on these is true thinking, then to contemplate the opposite of what Paul lists here, that is falsehood, dishonesty, injustice, impurity, unloveliness, is false thinking, or just thinking that we're thinking when in fact we're not thinking at all.

From the depth of his spiritual insight Christ Jesus explained the matter of true and false thinking by means of a parable (Mark 4: 3-20). He told of a sower sowing seed and that some fell among thorns where it was choked. Then he explained that the seed represented "the word" of God, and the thorns were the cares of the everyday world, the misleading hopes raised by riches, and general greed. He stated that those listeners who "hear the word, and receive it" will be fruitful—or, as we might say—will do useful, effective thinking and experience the good results of that thinking.

As a boy of twelve Jesus was able to talk with the learned men in the temple, and later men marveled how he came to have so much wisdom and learning. He ascribed all power to God, even his power to think; for he said, "Whatsoever I speak therefore, even as the Father said unto me, so I speak" (John 12:50). Obviously he equated true thinking with listening to the word of God, and failure to think with listening to the suggestions of evil. He rejected any suggestions of evil that came to him with such rebukes as "Get thee behind me, Satan."

We shall explore the nature of true thinking more deeply throughout the rest of our discussion, but it may be helpful if we consider first how we can best respond to Mrs. Eddy's urgent challenge that "the time for thinkers has come." How can this challenge be met in face of the general belief that evil is power? One means is by controlling the thoughts that come to us, admitting only thoughts from God, refusing entrance to suggestions of evil. So that we may understand this more clearly, let me give an example from my own life.

Controlling Our Own Thoughts

During a time of war I was captured overseas and imprisoned. It soon became evident that quite mistakenly I was being treated as a spy, and that my life was in danger. The realization of this brought me to my knees, and I prayed to God to be spared the experience of execution, promising that I would live my life to serve Him. In answer to this prayer it came to me, as if someone had spoken the words, "CONTROL THOUGHT!"

I knew at once this was a command for me to control my own thought, not somebody else's. And it was easy for me to recognize the source of this instruction to be God. It was fully in accord with Jesus' teaching, "When thou prayest, enter into thy closet, and when thou hast shut thy door, pray to thy Father which is in secret; and thy Father which seeth in secret shall reward thee openly" (Matt. 6:6).

It was in accord, too, with what I had learned in Christian Science about prayer, namely that we must shut the door of our consciousness against evil suggestions in order that it might be open to God's word. In short, controlling my own thought meant praying. And praying that wasn't just asking God to do something for me, but praying that meant thinking truly, deeply, spiritually. From that moment fearful suggestions, hateful suggestions, resentful suggestions were refused entrance to my consciousness. When they came—and they did come daily, even hourly—I absolutely refused to let them in.

At this time I was subjected to solitary confinement for three months, truly solitary, for in addition to not talking to others, or seeing others, I wasn't allowed to read. Thoughts were my only companions.

With a rusty old nail I scratched the letters C. T. on the wall of my cell as a constant reminder to control my thought. As wrong suggestions were barred from entering my thinking, divine thoughts began flooding my consciousness. This true thinking had an immediate effect upon me, physically as well as mentally. My body felt little discomfort, though there was no bed to sleep on and the temperature varied from extreme heat to the cold one experiences in tropical mountain regions.

I began to see thought as the actual substance of things. The battle was no longer with people and circumstances, but with false thinking, which was fast being corrected and defeated by true thinking. The sense of time was eliminated. These weren't long days dragging on in uncertainty and unhappiness, but rather periods filled with new glimpses of what Life really is. That it is God. And that man individually expresses this divine Life.

My mental struggles were at times severe, especially when I let the grimness of my empty cell, the barred window, and the miserable sounds around me impress themselves upon me. Nevertheless, it was daily becoming more apparent to me that my life wasn't in matter, that it wasn't dependent on a physical body, nor at the mercy of adverse or cruel circumstances. This life, I saw, could not be destroyed. I glimpsed the truth of the Biblical statement, ". . . in him we live, and move, and have our being" (Acts 17:28).

The Results of Controlling Thought

Gradually a deep sense of peace and calm assurance descended upon me. I finally remembered in its entirety this statement of Mrs. Eddy's, "Remember, thou canst be brought into no condition, be it ever so severe, where Love has not been before thee and where its tender lesson is not awaiting thee. Therefore despair not nor murmur, for that which seeketh to save, to heal, and to deliver, will guide thee, if thou seekest this guidance" (The First Church of Christ, Scientist, and Miscellany, p. 149).

To help keep my thought uplifted I sang hymns that I remembered from the Christian Science Hymnal. As days went by, my awareness of man's indestructible, immortal life in God, became clearer and clearer. Passages in the Bible were illumined in my thought, in particular the chapter in the book of Revelation in which St. John says of the holy city that "there shall be no more death, neither sorrow, nor crying, neither shall there be any more pain" (Rev. 21:4). I no longer thought of myself as being surrounded by enemies, but began to see all, in reality, as under the control of God.

Finally the day came when at the end of a period of questioning I was asked, "How do you feel about dying now?" I had become so inspired and uplifted through these months of prayer and the control of my thought that my answer seemed spoken for me. "You couldn't possibly kill me, for God, Spirit, created me spiritually; all you could do would be to do away with a dream about me. And if I were in your place, and you in mine, I couldn't kill you either; for the same God who created me spiritually, created you spiritually, and all I would be able to do would be to do away with a dream about you!"

Then came the last question, "Have you any wish?" Again as if the words were spoken for me, I answered, "Yes, I have, I wish to understand all about Life." I was then returned to my cell.

Some time later the interpreter came and announced that everything was going to be all right. Yet a week followed without food or water, except for one night when someone thrust the spout of a kettle through the bars of my window and poured water from it which I drank.

After this week of fasting, the same man, the officer-in-charge who previously had interrogated and threatened me, now came in with dishes of food, which he had prepared himself. At this time an offer was made to have a doctor come and examine me; but I was able to say that I was perfectly all right, that there had been no ill effects from the fasting. Afterwards I was lodged in a regular prisoner-of-war compound and I was well treated until my release. The fasting that had taken place was not only physical, but a mental and spiritual activity. Controlling my thought, listening for thoughts coming from God, had not only saved my life but had enabled me to keep well. Mrs. Eddy points out that, "Good thoughts are an impervious armor; clad therewith you are completely shielded from the attacks of error of every sort" (Miscellany, p. 210). This truly had been my experience.

Some Men Who Thought Truly

Now, I've illustrated at some length how it's possible to control our thinking even in extreme circumstances. Let's get back to the nature of true or right thinking. Just what is it and what effect does it have on us and others?

Early in our discussion we established that Paul's admonition to think on whatsoever things were virtuous and good would be correct thinking. Since God is the source of all good, He must also be the source of all good or right thoughts. So when these thoughts come to us we're in reality listening to God. Listening for the thoughts which flow from God is surely the essence of true thinking.

Many of the outstanding characters in the Bible had extraordinary ability to listen for thoughts coming from God. In the Old Testament men like Jacob, Moses, and Jeremiah heard such messages. They described these communications in statements like "Then the word of the Lord came to me, saying" (Jer. 18: 5), or simply as "And God said" (Gen. 9:12). All these men heard God's thoughts when they prayed. Their receptivity then resulted in clear direction for human action, such as when Moses was inspired to go to the Pharaoh and demand the release of the children of Israel from bondage.

Listening and praying are practically synonymous. Jesus' whole life was a prayer, a prayer of listening. Jesus always listened to the Father. He told his hearers "The word which ye hear is not mine, but the Father's which sent me" (John 14:24). Because of this, Jesus expressed, as fully as practical on the human scene, God's spiritual eternal nature. Therefore, he bore the title of Christ. The Christ, as we understand it, isn't a human person but the divine image or true idea of God, which Jesus so completely represented. The Christ is present and available to heal and save at all times and in all places. It's the Christ which enables us to listen to God and receive divine guidance. Let me tell you the result of spiritual listening in one man's experience. He was a Christian Scientist, and he was sitting in his study one night praying and listening. His home was in London. Suddenly he heard a thought to telephone a certain person in another country. At first he resisted, reasoning that a call to that country would be an unnecessary expenditure as there appeared to be no need for it. The thought persisted, however, with the added instruction to ask his friend to read Hymn 93 in the Christian Science Hymnal. This man had learned from experience to heed guidance that came through prayer, so he placed the call. Up to that point, though, he had no recollection of what Hymn 93 was about.

When the connection was made he was surprised to hear a strange voice at the other end inform him that his friend had just had a severe heart attack. When the caller requested that a message be taken, adding that he was speaking from London, he was told that his friend had been trying to scribble a message to someone in London, but that those around him were unable to decipher it. It was then suggested with some amazement that the caller might be the very one for whom the message was meant. This later proved to be the case.

The Christian Scientist had not only heard his friend's mental call, but also the direction to give him the hymn. His earnest prayer for his friend resulted in the healing of the heart condition, and the man was up and about the next day. You might be interested to know that the first verse of Hymn 93 reads:

> Happy the man whose heart can rest,
> Assured God's goodness ne'er will cease;
> Each day, complete, with joy is blessed,
> God keepeth him in perfect peace.

Many of you, I'm sure, have had such experiences. Then you'll know of another important element of the listening that is prayer; I refer to expectancy. When we pray, when we listen for God, we should be expectant of good. God means us to have all good, for He isn't a God of restriction, or limitation. God is infinite divine intelligence or Mind, expressing Himself through His idea, man, who has infinite good to enjoy. There are three things God will not let you have. They are sin, sickness, and death. All the rest, you can have. So expectancy of good is necessary to true thinking.

Only One Mind

If true thinking then consists of listening for thoughts coming from God, we must have access to these thoughts. So it's important that we establish our proper relationship to Him.

Man's relationship to God is the all-pervading theme in the Bible, especially in the New Testament, which deals chiefly with the teachings and works of Christ Jesus. Jesus showed God's relationship to us to be that of Father and beloved child. The Scriptures also tell us that man is the image and likeness of God. Man must, therefore, of necessity exactly express, or as we say, reflect, the qualities of God. God being Love, man must be loving. God being Truth, man must be truthful. God, being infinite and indestructible Spirit, man must be spiritual.

Divine Mind sends forth pure and wholesome thoughts, spiritual thoughts, that is, thoughts which aren't dependent on material considerations or determined by them. And one expressing such thoughts is said to be spiritually-minded. Listening to the suggestions of evil leads to the belief that mind is in matter and that there are many such minds, each expressing itself through a physical brain. But thinking spiritual thoughts leads us to the understanding that, because there's but one God, there is but one Mind. In listening to this one Mind only, we fulfill the First Commandment: "Thou shalt have no other gods before me" (Exodus 20:3).

The belief that we can outwit another, dominate or be dominated, springs from the supposition that each has a separate personal, finite mind, which can be both good and evil. When it's understood that there's but one Mind, one God, or good, only good can be experienced. And good will always shine through anyone whose thought is in rapport with the divine Mind.

For instance, no one who fully accepts the one Mind as man's only Mind can possibly experience lack; for this divine Mind constantly pours forth spiritual ideas, such as intelligence, and love. These are the substance of all supply, and they are ever available. You can prove this for yourselves, whatever your walk of life. An architect, using his intelligence, sees the transition from idea to paper, to actual form. In the resulting building we see the outward expression of service or usefulness, and whatever concept of beauty the architect has entertained. But the substance of these qualities is Spirit and they all have their source in divine Mind. Therefore they are ever present and inexhaustible. As Mrs. Eddy says, "God gives you His spiritual ideas, and in turn, they give you daily supplies" (Miscellaneous Writings, p. 307). What's true of our personal lives is true of world affairs, too.

Unsettled world conditions, wars, hatred, poverty, crime are the result of false thinking, the belief in many personal minds, some weak, some strong, some ignorant, some intelligent, some good, some evil. False suggestions present a world with millions of physical persons all thinking differently. True thinking reveals a universe controlled by Mind, God, and each one of us in our true being as God's idea expressing that one infinite Mind, God, good.

Thus each one of us reflects this Mind individually in infinite variety, but all are bound together by divine Love.

This is the relationship between God and man which we need to understand if we are to really think and not just think we think.

Mrs. Eddy, a True Thinker

I'm sure that you've been aware of my references to Mary Baker Eddy throughout our discussion. For over a hundred years Mrs. Eddy has been considered by the thousands of her followers, and by many who aren't her followers, as one of the great thinkers of all time.

We must realize that the stage of human events on which Mrs. Eddy appeared was filled with bright stars in the religious and intellectual world of nineteenth century America. There in New England, luminaries such as Ralph Waldo Emerson, Henry Thoreau, and Bronson Alcott sought to know and explain the meaning of nature, God, and man. In this atmosphere of intense religious and intellectual inquiry, Mrs. Eddy searched and studied, pursued lines of thought and experiment. Never far from her Bible and the teachings of Christ Jesus, she took particular note of his healing works. Finally when her spiritual insight and intuition were fully developed and prepared, she received from God the full revelation of scientific Christianity, of the Christ, Truth, which she has termed Christian Science.

In a letter dated 1876, Bronson Alcott wrote to Mrs. Eddy, 'The sacred truths which you announce sustained by facts of the Immortal Life, give to your work the seal of inspiration –reaffirm in modern phrase, the Christian revelations." It was indeed inspiration and revelation which enabled Mrs. Eddy to receive what Christian Scientists understand to be that other Comforter, that "Spirit of truth," which Jesus had promised.

As well as being the Discoverer of Christian Science and the author of many works on this subject, Mrs. Eddy established the Church of Christ, Scientist, with its Mother Church in Boston, Massachusetts, and its branches around the world. This church was founded by Mrs. Eddy to promote, protect, and foster her discovery. It is today leavening the thinking of mankind with the true idea of God and of His reflection, man.

Mrs. Eddy was a true spiritual thinker, who listened for thoughts, ideas, coming from God. She was able to detect and bar evil suggestions; and to listen for the impartations of the divine Mind. But beyond this, she gives guidance to all who desire to bring their thinking under control—to replace false thinking with true thinking, thinking which expresses thoughts from God. In effect, she accepted her own challenge that "the time for thinkers has come."

A Defense Against Brainwashing

We've now considered what false thinking claims to be and what true thinking really is. We should now be able to identify whether we just think we think, that is, listen to false suggestions, or whether we really think, that is, listen for and assimilate true thoughts from the divine Mind, God.

Merely identifying each type of mental activity, however, isn't sufficient. To experience the full effect of right thinking we must really stay with it.

In the first place, true and good thoughts from God, vigorously entertained, will prevent our being hypnotized, as it were, by evil suggestions. Right thinking defends us from all forms of brainwashing, blatant or subtle. Hypnotic suggestions are counterfeits of true thoughts, thoughts coming from God. They are a state of sleep, rather than of awareness.

The more obvious forms of suggestions are sometimes found in advertising. I hardly need give you an example but let me cite just one. There's a TV commercial which shows the pendulum of a clock swinging back and forth while a voice keeps on repeating the word "pain." Markets are sometimes created for products by mental suggestion, especially in the field of drugs and patent medicine. Suggestion, that approaches hypnotism, is too often used in sales campaigns, and various forms of mental manipulation are widespread. Advertising, properly used, performs a valuable service to the community but our thinking needs to be protected from aggressive intrusion.

Sometimes such influences take a less noticeable form. This is illustrated in the story about Mrs. Wiggs of the Cabbage Patch whose husband I believe was a ne'er-do-well. She kept excusing his lack of ambition which others ascribed to sheer laziness, with the assertion that he was a deep thinker, and in this way she defended his lack of ambition. One time when a visitor was present, right in the middle of a conversation, our Mr. Wiggs dozed off. Mrs. Wiggs quite equal to the situation exclaimed, "Oh, he has thunk himself to sleep."

Have some of us at times "thunk" ourselves to sleep, perhaps even during those times when we're seeking greater spiritual enlightenment—such as during a church service? I have. But this is the counterfeit of thinking, robbing us of the good which God is always ready to impart. It's this same counterfeit thinking, this same hypnotic influence which robbed Jesus' disciples of witnessing his struggle and glory in the Garden of Gethsemane. The disciples were put to sleep, in other words, they ceased thinking. To allow ourselves to be put to sleep mentally would rob us of the precious experience of spiritual progress—the result of real thinking.

We Can Protect Our Thinking

But what if we feel we're not able to control our thinking and put out the suggestions of worry, anxiety, fear? Is there anything we can do? We can do something very concrete. We can stop believing a lie. The seeming inability to control our thinking stems from the belief in the power and reality of evil. Evil has no power or reality! It's only a lying belief, a suggestion that it's powerful and real and that we must accept it into our thoughts. But as *Science and Health* stresses, "You must control evil thoughts in the first instance, or they will control you in the second" (p. 234).

Because God, infinite good, is All-in-all, we understand evil in all its forms to be unreal, that is, like a dream or illusion without substance or permanence. But this needs to be proved by each one individually by making sure that his life is governed by God. To ensure that our lives are governed and guided by God, we need to detect evil and outwit it. We can do this by always remembering that evil's claim is an illusion. That evil is hypnotic and all suggestions of evil that present themselves as our thinking are a form of brainwashing.

Evil thoughts purposely directed at us can have no effect on us if we exercise control over our thinking, over what we listen to and accept. No one can inject thoughts into our consciousness if we set up a barrier of good and true thoughts. This protection extends into the time we spend in sleep as well as through our waking hours.

At this point let me refer back to my war experience. All during the three months of solitary confinement I slept well except for one night. This particular night I was awakened with the feeling that my mentality was being tampered with and that I should stay awake, and spiritually defend myself. This I did through prayer, through filling my consciousness with thoughts from God. After some time the feeling suddenly ceased, as if a faucet had been turned off.

I forgot all about the incident until just before the end of hostilities when a man was brought into the compound who said he knew me. He was a native of the occupied country, and had been employed at the prison where I had been kept in solitary confinement. It seems he had been present the night when my captors had been attempting to subject me to mental manipulation, or suggestion, for the purpose of questioning me later. The reason he remembered me well, he said, was that this attempt at mental tampering had had no effect on me. He was so impressed, he had noted my name, rank, and service number.

Even today sinister mental influences are at work to make us lose faith in good, in morality, and in common decency. We are bombarded with all kinds of evil suggestions telling us that a laissez-faire attitude toward all kinds of conduct is right, modern, and normal. Such false thinking and its resultant woes spell out slavery, both mental and physical. But on the other side great moral and spiritual forces are also being felt. These are releasing mankind from slavery and bringing good. Our part is to respond to them, to listen for what they tell us, to think truly.

Never Too Late

In my particular wartime experiences I have spoken of control of my thought as a refusal to let fear, hatred, resentment and evil suggestions of other kinds to enter my consciousness—to get a foothold at all in my thinking.

However, in our everyday living we may have sometimes permitted an evil suggestion to enter and occupy our thought for a period—for days, months, even years. This wrong thinking may have taken the form of remembrance of past grievances or injustice, or criticism of the actions of friends or family. Whatever its form may be, we can be sure that such thinking will rob us in some way, unless we uproot and eliminate it. And it's never too late to do this.

During my war experience, when it was a matter of life and death, it was imperative to control my thoughts. However, when back in civilian life, I once let my guard down badly.

Through a freak accident, I found myself in pretty bad shape. My left arm became completely useless and I suffered excruciating pain throughout my left side. The symptoms became so alarming that the friends with whom I was staying became concerned for me. They weren't Christian Scientists, and without my knowledge called a physician. When I became aware of what was happening, I heard the verdict that my arm would remain useless as there was no known cure for that condition. I heard the verdict but I didn't listen to it. Instead I roused myself to examine my thinking in the light of Christian Science.

It dawned on me that this wasn't just a physical condition but that I had permitted discouragement, resentment, self-pity, and fear to take hold of my thought. An attractive position had been offered me, but hadn't materialized. This had been a severe blow to me since I had left my former position. I saw that my unhappy mental state had resulted in my bodily injury and its alarming results. This analysis proved to be correct. As I set about eliminating fear, self-pity, resentment, and discouragement and replacing these with love, forgiveness, courage, and trust in God, I was entirely healed. I also found suitable employment. Another statement from *Science and Health* had been proved in my experience, namely this: "Is it not well to eliminate from so-called mortal mind that which, so long as it remains in mortal mind, will show itself in forms of sin, sickness, and death?" (p. 348).

Evil cannot endure in our experience when our thought dwells on God, divine good, and on His idea, man. We can prove for ourselves that by entertaining pure and wholesome thoughts we cannot remain the victim of sin, sickness, or slavery of any sort, for good will always be established in the lives of those who are willing to think truly.

Emerging from the debris of war, social evils, and racial strife is a new-old ideal, which has gripped the imagination of men everywhere. Everywhere men are feeling the urge for individual self-expression, and to be recognized as having human dignity. This ideal cannot be stifled, and as it develops a new race will inevitably appear. This will be a race of thinkers.

WHAT ARE YOUR DIMENSIONS FOR LIVING?

What Are Your Dimensions for Living?

John H. Wyndham, C.S.B.

Once during a film expedition into the heart of Equatorial Africa I met a boy named Modjena. He was the son of a village chief and was about twelve years old.

In this part of the world, births aren't recorded; they're usually related to events such as a famine, feast or plague. Even nature is hostile. There's the wilderness in which the sun beats down fiercely by day, and nights are filled with the sounds of wild animals. As you can gather, Modjena's dimensions for living were quite rugged.

I was making a documentary film of this area and Modjena was in it. He participated with intelligence and enthusiasm, responding easily to directions given by signs and examples. When I asked him, through an interpreter, what he'd like as a reward, he unhesitatingly pointed to my clothing.

I explained that such things went with another way of life such as living in a town, working at a job. Modjena insisted that he wanted the clothing, *especially* the shoes. And so we journeyed by jeep to a place where such things could be purchased. You never saw such bright eyes and winning smile when we found a pair of shoes to fit him.

Six months later, after I'd returned to Europe, I met the Swiss doctor who'd previously been our guide. He'd again visited the area and told me Modjena was in school. A whole new dimension for living had opened up for him. And, by the way, he was wearing shoes.

Haven't most of us, like Modjena, at times longed for a new dimension to our living? One of better opportunities, better health, happiness, and security—entirely satisfying, fulfilling our most cherished hopes and aspirations? In fact, in these revolutionary times, the demand for new dimensions has reached an all-time high and has taken various directions.

For example, some in today's new generation feel that a material sense of life has too long fooled their elders. They no longer respect wealth and social status, but have become deeply concerned for the people they see suffering from poverty and disease in distant countries or from lack and deprivation right here in our own land.

Unfortunately, another direction taken by these seeking a new dimension causes great concern. There are those who through drugs try to escape life's problems or to expand their minds so as to become aware, as they say, of new spiritual experiences. Some even claim they can find God that way.

Discovery of a New Dimension

Over the years, various enlightened individuals have looked for new dimensions. During the latter half of the last century, mathematicians explored quite a number of these. Then in 1895, the British novelist, H. G. Wells, in his book *The Time Machine*, discussed the theory that time is a fourth dimension to the three-dimensional space humans live in. Ten years later, Professor Albert Einstein published his Special Theory of Relativity in which he developed the idea of a four-dimensional space-time continuum. As you might suppose, all these men were concerned with mathematical or physical dimensions.

Yet, contemporary with Wells and Einstein was another individual who was also looking for an extra dimension, a quite different one, the dimension of Spirit. In 1896, the year after H. G. Wells first popularized his idea of a fourth dimension, an article appeared in *The Granite Monthly* entitled, "One Cause and Effect." In it the Discoverer of Christian Science, Mary Baker Eddy, wrote, "Christian Science translates Mind, God, to mortals. It is the infinite calculus defining the line, plane, space, and fourth dimension of Spirit" (Miscellaneous Writings, p. 22). It's with this concept that we're concerned today.

Mrs. Eddy not only discovered this extra dimension; she wrote a book about it, *Science and Health with Key to the Scriptures.* Here she presents this revolutionary concept of the universe and man. She writes: "The compounded minerals or aggregated substances composing the earth, the relations which constituent masses hold to each other, the magnitudes, distances and revolutions of the celestial bodies, are of no real importance, when we remember that they all must give place to the spiritual fact by the translation of man and the universe back into Spirit. In proportion as this is done, man and the universe will be found harmonious and eternal" (p.209).

In these thought-provoking words we're directed to look beyond the concept of the universe as material or as both material and mental. Instead we're invited to become conscious of the truly scientific fact of a wholly spiritual universe and a wholly spiritual man. As we respond to this invitation, we begin the translation of man and the universe back into Spirit. We begin to replace each material object in our surroundings with the spiritual fact that the material object either symbolizes or counterfeits.

In the measure we do this, we'll find the universe and ourselves, our whole experience, becoming progressively more harmonious.

How Mrs. Eddy Made the Discovery

Now just what is the nature of this spiritual dimension Mrs. Eddy discovered and where is it to be found? First let me give you a little background.

At a time when women had few rights, when opportunities for women to enter business were almost nil, this woman had a burning desire to find the law by which Jesus of Nazareth invoked health and sustenance.

As a sincere Christian, she believed in divine healing. And under conditions which would have discouraged the bravest of us, she searched for and finally discovered the Science which Jesus used to heal. She opened up a whole new dimension for living with unlimited possibilities for good.

Mrs. Eddy proved this in her own life. From ill health and weakness she rose to the demonstration of extraordinary capacity and endurance. She became the only woman ever to establish a great religion. Today it encircles the globe. In addition to writing *Science and Health* and other books on Christian Science, she founded the Church of Christ, Scientist, with its many and varied activities. Finally, at the age of 87, she established an international daily newspaper now read by presidents, heads of state, and people of many nationalities around the world. Many of you here have probably read an issue of *The Christian Science Monitor*.

Mrs. Eddy's discovery and accomplishments stand as a beacon for all who wish to experience a new dimension.

Jesus Showed What the Spiritual Dimension Is

Now as to the nature of this spiritual dimension and where it's to be found, let's turn first of all to the Bible, and in particular to the works and teachings of Christ Jesus. It was her study of these that so largely prepared Mrs. Eddy to make her discovery. The life of Jesus clearly demonstrated the existence of an extra dimension beyond the three dimensions of height, depth, and breadth usually accepted by us. One extraordinary example of this is shown in the Gospel of Matthew, Chapter 17.

As it is related there, Jesus took three of his most promising disciples, Peter, James, and John. And the four of them climbed a mountain. There they had a mind-expanding experience beyond compare. His disciples saw Jesus transfigured. They actually saw him change his form—enter, we may say, another dimension. They saw and heard him speaking with Moses and Elias, both of whom had passed from the human scene many hundreds of years before.

At that moment were not man and the universe translated back into Spirit by Jesus? Didn't he show the existence of a universe where time is not and where man has his identity and individuality in the realm of Spirit—where man is seen not to be material and transient but an eternal spiritual idea in the divine Mind which is God?

The Bible records that during his transfiguration or translation into another dimension, Jesus' garments shone white with whiteness "as no fuller on earth"—no material cleansing medium—"can white them" (Mark 9:3) This symbolism indicates that it's spiritual purity which enables us to enter the dimension of Spirit. We can begin to do this now. But before the dimension of Spirit can open to us completely, we need to have spiritual purity, pure spiritual sense—pure from the limitation of time and space and physical existence.

Jesus rebuked the Pharisees and other formalists of his time and ours with stinging words such as "Ye are like unto whited sepulchres, which indeed appear beautiful outward, but are within full . . . of all uncleanness" (Matt 23:27). The dead form of religion without the healing Christ made manifest in wholesome human lives is certainly not the vibrant teaching of the Master. He clearly pointed the way for all with such words as, "But the hour cometh, and now is, when the true worshippers shall worship the Father in spirit and in truth" (John 4:23).

Jesus knew that the belief of life as material must be wholly rejected. Increasing spirituality and progressive rejection of material concepts can finally lead us into that extra dimension for living—the dimension where man and the universe are found translated back into Spirit.

Christ, the Door to Spiritual Dimension

I spoke just now of the healing Christ.

Now let's look a little deeper into why, prior to Mrs. Eddy's discovery of the Science of Christ, men didn't enter more fully into the dimension of Spirit—that state of consciousness where sickness, lack, sorrow, and death don't exist.

About 1900 years ago Jesus, and in a good measure his disciples, had known how to use spiritual means to feed the hungry and heal sickness. Even the dead were raised and grief gave place to rejoicing. Then over two or three centuries this knowledge was lost. It would appear this inability to follow Jesus in his demonstration of spiritual power is largely due to a misunderstanding of the nature of the Christ. The discovery of Christian Science has restored the Christ to its proper status.

In this Science Jesus is rightly identified as Jesus the Christ or Christ Jesus. No condition could separate him from the Christ. He is the human being who at every point of his career most fully represented the Christ by the completeness of his expression of God. But the Christ is much more than any single human being. The Christ is the true idea of God, of divine Life, Truth, and Love, of divine Mind and Spirit, of all that God is or includes, of the universe and man translated back into Spirit. This true idea of all reality has always existed long before the human Jesus trod the earth. Jesus said, referring to the eternal Christ, "Before Abraham was, I am" (John 8:58).

It is this eternal Christ, this true idea of God, that we can all express. In so doing we translate each detail of our human experience back into its spiritual original. Step by step the Christ, Truth, leads us to find our spiritual universe and our spiritual being, independent of matter—our being as the sons and daughters of God. Then expressing the Christ to the best of our ability, we're able to understand Jesus' words and follow his healing example. We're able in ever greater degree to enter, explore, and experience "the fourth dimension of Spirit," where there's no lack, no shortage of anything needed for our well-being—for all men's well-being.

It has already been proved by thousands that some understanding of the dimension of Spirit has healed their ills and woes, and has opened up a whole new world of possibilities for them.

The Dimension of Spirit Practical in Daily Life

Now just how are our lives affected by this new scientific knowledge of the dimension of Spirit? And where is it to be found? It's to be found where it has always been—within our own consciousness.

Referring to this spiritual dimension, Jesus said, "The kingdom of God cometh not with observation: Neither shall they say, Lo here! or, Lo there! for, behold, the kingdom of God is within you"

(Luke 17:20, 21). Men haven't found this kingdom of God within, because they've believed themselves to be material, subject to sin, sickness, and death. Only by the translation of man and the universe back into Spirit can this kingdom, this dimension of Spirit, be realized.

And let me add, this dimension isn't just an optimistic outlook. It's a realization of spiritual good right where the physical senses claim there's inharmony, sickness, and all kinds of limiting conditions. This realization of spiritual good goes hand in hand with the experiencing, yes, the actual possession of such things as health, happiness, and security. Let me illustrate from my own life.

As a boy of about twelve, I used to daydream of a place where all was beauty and harmony. I fancied that it lay somewhere where the sun went down below the horizon. We lived in a small European country not far from where a fierce war was raging. And I was in a constant state of fear and insecurity. Severe headaches and chronic depression were almost daily occurrences. As a result my school grades were often unsatisfactory. I was perplexed about the meaning of life, a life which to me seemed cruel and sad.

But on a happier note were the times when my grandmother read to me from a children's Bible. These experiences initiated my search for a religion that could clarify God to me. I well remember at one time it led me to a sixteenth-century church where I sat on a hard wooden bench trying to read the inscriptions on the tombstones which formed the floor of the church. The preacher thundered hellfire and brimstone at us, predicting everlasting punishment for all sinners. Even for the best of us he held out little hope, for as he said, we were all born in sin. I was shocked and startled, but nevertheless continued my search.

A Search Is Rewarded

Then one day circumstances made it necessary for me to live with relatives in the United States. I found my schoolbook English completely inadequate either to understand or effectively communicate with anyone. Everyone seemed to be talking at such a furious rate. But some time later a man offered me a book, which he said would teach me English in a wonderful way. I'll always remember his face for it shone with such love and compassion.

With the help of a dictionary, I commenced to read. I was enthralled. Here was a book filled with new ideas on what life really is, what God is, and what man is. New concepts and ideas literally jumped out of the pages. This book was *Science and Health*. And it not only taught me English—it also opened up a whole new dimension of health, hope, and faith for me.

With what I learned from this book, my thinking began to change radically. God, I found, wasn't a God who punished men for sins He made them capable of committing. I learned that God is divine Principle, Life, Truth, and Love, the creator of a perfect spiritual universe of which the material is merely an inversion, or at best a symbol. Most important, I began to see man, not as a mortal living precariously in a physical body, which can give him some pleasure and a whole lot of pain—I began to see man as God's spiritual child destined to enjoy all the good his heavenly Father has already bestowed on him.

I soon grasped the idea that the real man is spiritual and perfect. That man is the immortal expression of God, Spirit, expressing His attributes and qualities, all good. As the translation of man and the universe back into Spirit became part of my thinking, unhappy fearful thinking gave way to trustful happy thinking. My periods of depression began to vanish and were replaced with enlightened expectation of good. Life no longer seemed one headache after another, and so my suffering from nervous headaches ceased and gave place to health and freedom. The unhappy memory of failing in school was erased as I learned that God is man's true source of intelligence. This understanding later enabled me to pass examinations with high grades.

Through the revelations of Christian Science, through the translation of man and the universe back into Spirit, I found my place of beauty and harmony right over the horizon. That is, I found it right over the horizon of material limited thinking and living, in the glorious dimension of Spirit.

And something I'd been eager for since my grandmother read to me from the children's Bible—I gained an understanding of the true meaning of Jesus' lifework. It pointed to the wholly new dimension for living which I was now beginning to discover.

Abundance Part of Spiritual Dimension

Once we begin to understand even a little of the Science demonstrated by Jesus, and revealed by Mrs. Eddy, we too can enter to some degree into that dimension of Spirit, to which Jesus had free access.

Consider the incident in the Bible when 5,000 men besides women and children needed food and were fed when only a few loaves and fishes were available. What took place here? What did Jesus do and teach his disciples, and us, through his example? The disciples were unable to feed the multitude. They experienced the limitations of matter. Christ Jesus by utilizing the infinite calculus of Spirit proved the existence of a limitless dimension, where no so-called adverse laws of matter exist—only the law of Spirit, divine Love, whereby man's every need is fully supplied.

The disciples, from their point of limited spiritual development, could only calculate within the framework of their material three-dimensional concept of being. Consequently, they calculated that five loaves and two fishes couldn't possibly provide for 5,000 men, besides women and children. From their standpoint of limitation their calculation appeared correct.

Jesus, however, revealed a limitless dimension and used the infinite calculus of Spirit to multiply good. This resulted, as the Bible records, in an abundance of food.

A Modern Demonstration of Abundance

Let me tell you how some understanding of these same truths once helped me in a threatening situation.

I was engaged to manage a business which had suffered many reverses. One payday not long after I had started, there wasn't any money in the bank to pay the salaries. In the privacy of my office, I prayed earnestly to quiet my fears. I remember saying to God that I couldn't possibly accept the responsibility for employees having to go home to their families without money for food and other necessities. So I had to throw my burden on Him while affirming my faith in His willingness and ability to care for all. I denied the suggestion that any of God's children could lack or be embarrassed. Hadn't Jesus proved this with the loaves and the fishes?

About 2:30 the girl whose job it was to go to the bank came with the payroll check for me to sign. I said that I would call when I was ready, and continued praying. I raised my thought into that spiritual dimension where I had learned that man forever dwells as the beloved child of God.

About a quarter of three the girl came again. Time was short, she said, and could she have the check? Again, I had to ask her to wait. This time I really had to vehemently deny the suggestions of fear and failure and strongly claim God's presence and allness. Minutes before three, the girl appeared again together with a messenger boy. She could just make it to the bank, she said. Then the boy spoke up. His boss had sent him around with a check, which, although not due, he thought I might like to have. It was an advance on work we were doing. You can imagine with what gratitude I signed the salary check. I then asked the girl to deposit the other check at the same time. It was from a nationally known company and would be honored on sight. From that day the company increased in prosperity, enlarging its scope and usefulness all along the line. In the realm of Spirit, God's tender care is ever present to meet the individual human need.

Solving the World's Problems in the Dimension of Spirit

Now the divine Principle that operated for me on that day when no hope of supplying the needs of my employees seemed possible, can be applied to all phases of human need. This Principle, demonstrated so fully by Jesus and again fully available through Christian Science, is adequate to solve all earth's problems lovingly and effectively.

Let me just deal briefly with two major world problems crying out for an urgent solution. Each of these, like all the other human problems today, demands that we enter the dimension of Spirit.

We have, for instance, urgent need to solve bad social and moral conditions. There's the problem of drug addiction which today is a major cause for men's degeneration, immorality, and lawlessness. Some modern writers and thinkers see today's widespread use of drugs as part of the spread of mystic religions and philosophies promising the expansion of one's consciousness. But through such influence men are pulled down and debased rather than uplifted. Others are merely saddened, made hopeless or confused. We've all heard of the gruesome murders, the suicides, the broken lives as the price paid for drug-taking, of the hopeless parents whose children have left home, victims of the drug habit and all that this stands for. In New York City alone there are an estimated 25,000 young addicts, and well over 200 teenagers died there last year from heroin-related infections.

Each and every one of these parents in despair would do almost anything to find an antidote to this murderous evil. True scientific Christianity alone is able to destroy this degenerating influence. It can expand men's consciousness through spiritual truths to reach the knowledge of their true identity as the children of God, as individual spiritual ideas of the divine Mind.

The groundwork for the drug problem we're facing today would appear to have been laid over past centuries. Robert E. Gould, a New York physician, writes in an article entitled "Drug Abuse," "We ourselves have created the drug problem. Witness our nicotine habit (cigarette smoking), our caffeine habit (coffee), and our addiction to alcohol. Millions of us regularly consume barbiturates, tranquilizers, and amphetamines (often as 'diet' pills). The picture is plain: Few of us can deny excessive reliance on drugs in our daily lives. That our drugs may not be marijuana, LSD, or other psychedelics which the young favor is beside the point. The point is that we adults have set patterns of drug abuse for the young to follow." (PTA Magazine, March, 1970).

This drug-taking over the years appears to have encouraged people to look on virtually all drugs as being beneficial. The corner drug-store has played its part in conditioning human thinking to believe that drugs are a necessary part of life.

The Healing Power of Divine Mind

Christian Science reverses the belief that we can't live without drug-taking. It shows that health and well-being and true expansion of consciousness result from the application of the power of divine Mind. As one woman told me: "I've come for help in Christian Science. The doctor to whom I turned told me: 'Go to the Christian Scientists. They deal with causes, we only deal with effects.' " The power of divine Mind reaches recesses of consciousness to which the most potent drug can never penetrate.

To illustrate how God's help can be effectively sought in cases of hopeless illness, let me tell you of one who was told by doctors that she couldn't live unless two kinds of drugs were taken twice a day.

This person had been taken into our home to be in an atmosphere where she might work out her problem in Christian Science.

The picture at first was grim; we had much to do to eliminate fear and let go a heavy sense of responsibility. The patient hungrily studied the Bible and *Science and Health* seeking to be released from the bondage of drugs. This prepared her for taking some practical mental and spiritual steps.

The first attempt to quit drugs, however, failed. Then it was seen that there was a deep sense of resentment, a resentment so fierce that it flooded her consciousness. In consequence, the disease had literally flooded her body, threatening to cut off breath and life. When the mental root of the disease was seen, the patient made another attempt to do without the drugs. This time there was success, because her thought had been lifted into the realm where man is seen as cared for by God, and not at the mercy of misfortune and injustice. For years now she has been living wholly free from drugs and in good health.

To those thousands who are seeking new dimensions through drug-taking or are taking drugs for any other reason, Christian Science says: "Come and be healed. Know and understand and prove your true relationship to God. Begin to live in the dimension of Spirit."

One God, One Christ, Unites All Men

Spiritual living can solve another problem requiring our earnest attention. The race question.

Scientific inventions in communications, together with speed in travel, have made our world too small to live in racial isolation, and men are forced to find a solution to their racial bias. The translation of man and the universe back into Spirit offers here the real solution, in fact the only solution. It shows men's real nature and character to be universally good, pure, and wholesome, because wholly spiritual. It proves that men have a common spiritual origin as the sons and daughters of God made in His likeness.

This spiritually scientific fact is in sharp contrast to what the physical senses say: That men are divided by race, color, and creed, and therefore are natural enemies, or at best suspiciously tolerate each other.

At one time it was my experience to be a prisoner of war, the captive of a people of different color and physical structure, a people whose culture and religion I didn't understand. At first my world seemed to have completely collapsed. Strange customs and strange mental forces tended to confuse. Then there was the threatening despair caused by the prevalent suggestion that the war would last twenty years and we would never be freed—that only imprisonment and subjection awaited us.

We were often subjected to what my fellow officers considered indignities; but I felt no resentment. Always the idea of living in another, a spiritual, dimension stayed with me. It enabled me to maintain an abiding consciousness of care and protection, where around me appeared fear, hopelessness, and suffering.

I'd volunteered to work as overseer of some two hundred soldiers on a farm outside the prison camp. The vegetables grown there were distributed to different camps. As time went by, the morale and the health of many of the prisoners became steadily worse. Food was insufficient and the things which were considered necessary to a proper diet weren't available.

A Christmas of Spirit

That year, just before Christmas, I was asked by the camp doctor if I would try and persuade the farm commandant to purchase quantities of fruit in the nearby villages. He said this might help save the lives of some prisoners suffering from beri-beri and other diseases. For this purpose money had been collected and I was given a small roll of notes, or bills as you call them, to pay for the fruit should I be successful.

Praying as to how I might approach this matter, I made my way to the hut where the commandant was. As I stood there before his desk, his expression conveyed that I would never get through to him. Then the thought came, "Tell him about Christmas." In a mixture of languages, I conveyed, as best I could, the meaning of Christmas, as I understood it in Christian Science. I spoke of the Christ-idea, of men's true brotherhood, of love and goodwill toward men. I asked to have much fruit brought so that Christmas might have real meaning for those sick in the camp.

All this time I was met with stony silence. There seemed not a flicker of comprehension or sympathy. As a last attempt I repeated some of the thoughts I had tried to convey and put the roll of money on the desk. The money, however, was swept brusquely aside. I left with not a single clue as to what had been understood of my plea. But I still refused to feel disappointment or resentment. I knew that I and all men, both captives and captors, truly lived in the dimension of Spirit.

Some days later when making the rounds of the field, a very excited guard on a bicycle came riding towards me gesturing and shouting to me to come at once. He began pushing me in the back to make me run, shouting in French, "Courez, courez!"—"Run, run!" My first thought was that another beating was taking place somewhere and that my presence was required. However, I was shunted to the commandant's hut and told to go inside. There behind his desk was the commandant, a broad grin on his face, and on the floor around him several natives squatting beside huge baskets full of fruit.

Astonished and grateful I stepped forward and put the roll of money I was still carrying with me on the desk. Again it was brusquely swept aside, but this time I could hardly believe my eyes and ears. Pointing at his chest, the commandant repeated, "Kismis, Kismis." And with that he took money out of his pocket and paid for the fruit.

I can tell you that day the men made a joyful entrance into the camp pushing a cart loaded with the fruit. The Christ-spirit was really felt that Christmas. Even the guards seemed to take part in the excitement. Yes, the Christ-Spirit had broken through the barriers of race, hate, and despair. All men truly have one Father. It's the Christ which bridges the gap men have placed between themselves, and between themselves and God.

Racial strife and hatred are doomed to be extinguished, for the Christ knocks at the door of humanity insisting on its universal acceptance. Through a scientific sense of the Christ, men will find a new dimension for living together in universal brotherhood, seeing each other as they really are, God's spiritual ideas.

The Final Achievement

Isn't what the world is really crying out for today, a whole new dimension for living? And isn't this the question for us all today: Are we going to dream along believing we live in matter and fearfully suffer it out, or are we going to translate man and the universe back into Spirit and gloriously live it out free from hate, sin, disease, and death?

Christian Science today calls to all men in these words from *Science and Health*: "Through discernment of the spiritual opposite of materiality, even the way through Christ, Truth, man will reopen with the key of divine Science the gates of Paradise which human beliefs have closed, and will find himself unfallen, upright, pure, and free, not needing to consult almanacs for the probabilities either of his life or of the weather, not needing to study brainology to learn how much of a man he is. Mind's control over the universe, including man, is no longer an open question, but is demonstrable Science" (p. 171).

The first man to step on the noon, Neil Armstrong, has expressed the hope that in this age men will come to understand the universe around them—that men will come to understand themselves! Men have trod the moon. But they can go further! They can walk with God in the free and limitless dimension of Spirit.

THE DIVINE ADVENTURE

The Divine Adventure

John H. Wyndham, C.S.B.

My earliest recollections of adventure take me back to a village on the lovely river Vecht in my native Holland. There was a small castle in the village, surrounded by a high wall. Through the enormous wrought-iron gates opening up to a driveway, one could see a stately mansion.

Each year on the 5th of December an extraordinary person with a flowing white beard would ride through the gates on a white horse and proceed up the main street. On his head he wore a high pointed miter embroidered with a golden cross, and he held a golden staff in his hand. He wore a red velvet cape that even covered part of the horse. I was told he was a saint who had come from sunny Spain.

His servant was clothed like a medieval page boy. He would dig his hand into a large heavy sack for tiny toys, small round ginger cookies, and nuts. With the other children I would reach out respectfully. We were awed by the mysterious saint and his servant Peter who were supposed to know whether we had been good or naughty. To me this occurrence was high adventure.

At another time a group of gypsies passed through my village. They had gaudy horse-drawn wagons and many dogs and even monkeys. As they passed they played on flutes, banged tambourines, and sang. They had colorful clothes, and the women wore large earrings. Many small children were with them.

That day I didn't come home at evening, and my parents finally had to get the village policeman to find me. I had followed the gypsies and, spellbound, had watched them make camp outside the village. Again adventure had come into my life.

My third glimpse of adventure occurred when I was told there were some strange people and animals beyond a wall just behind my home. I climbed to the top of the wall and peered over. In a convent garden, I spotted an extraordinary animal with a very lovable but comical face. It had a large hump on its back and very long legs. The man who attended it was wrapped in white clothing which covered his head. The strangeness of this scene fascinated me and I speculated what kind of animal and what kind of person these might be. For a while after these adventures, when I went to bed my imagination wandered through exotic lands where saints and gypsies and camels came from.

Then the war burst over Europe. For a time my adventures were forgotten. Although my country remained neutral, talk among grown-ups became serious and people didn't smile. They were afraid.

During these years I learned about misfortune firsthand as I saw the terror of refugees and stood in long lines for our small ration of food.

By the time I reached twelve, I also saw my early adventures in a different light. I'd found out the man on the white horse with the miter and scepter wasn't really a saint from Spain, but a kindly benefactor of my village playing Saint Nicholas. The gypsies weren't really such happy people, but nomads who got shunted from village to village. The man with the camel, I learned, came from a land where there was great poverty. Although my thirst for adventure remained, I no longer felt that all was as romantic as I'd first believed. But I still hoped for a place to go of real adventure—away from fear, war, and human unhappiness, a place of peace.

The words "divine adventure" in the title of this lecture I've taken from a letter of greeting by Mary Baker Eddy, the Discoverer and Founder of Christian Science. The occasion was the laying of the cornerstone of First Church of Christ, Scientist, in her home city of Concord, New Hampshire. She wrote to the church members, "We live in an age of Love's divine adventure to be All-in-all." (The First Church of Christ, Scientist and Miscellany, p. 158)

This Love she speaks of is actually a synonym for God. St. John says in one of his letters to the early Christian churches, "God is love." It's the infinite nature, the allness, of God, Love, that, when understood and demonstrated in our daily living, gives us the experience of the highest adventure possible—divine adventure.

Throughout the Bible there are many indications that God, besides being infinite Love is also infinite wisdom, intelligence, Mind. In the New Testament the Apostle Paul speaks of this divine Mind as "the Mind of Christ" and "the Mind that was in Christ Jesus." God, as scientifically understood, is certainly infinite intelligence.

This brings me to one of the cardinal points I want to make tonight. If our life of adventure isn't to be chancy, isn't to contain the possibility of becoming misadventure, or misfortune, it must be directed and controlled by a God who not only is divine Love—but who is also divine Mind, divine intelligence, and who includes all the specific qualities that make up true intelligence.

We'll see, as we go along, it's the fallible human mind that causes us to experience misadventure and the divine Mind which provides us with a life of true adventure—specifically in regard to health and our expectations of the future.

Distinguishing Divine Mind from Human Mind

In her book *Science and Health with Key to the Scriptures*, p.82, Mrs. Eddy writes: "In a world of sin and sensuality hastening to a greater development of power, it is wise earnestly to consider whether it is the human mind or the divine Mind which is influencing one."

So in our search for true adventure we need to be able first of all to distinguish between the human mind and the divine Mind. Frequently God is charged with causing all sorts of evil—earthquakes, floods, devastating cyclones, yes, even the untimely death of a child, a man or a woman. A false sense of theology sees such things as the will of God, who, although He is infinite Love, still is supposed to punish His children and treat them cruelly. This kind of illogical and misguided thinking takes place in the human mind, often right but just as often wrong, certainly undependable. This type of thinking appears to see both good and evil. It's what Jesus referred to as the field where tares and wheat grew side by side. To refer back to my childhood adventures, it was mistaken human thinking that saw adventure in the man on the white horse, the gypsies, and the man with the camel.

Mrs. Eddy equates the human mind with mortal mind when speaking of its transitory, limited nature. This mind, if allowed to govern our human experience, acts out unpredictable as well as predictable evil consequences. When indulged in to any extent, it becomes uncontrollable and results in gross inharmony, such as moral idiocy, crime, and war. It's the kind of thinking St. Paul called the carnal or fleshly mind.

Such are the errors of the human, or mortal mind. What now are the characteristics of divine Mind? Mind, as a synonym for God, denotes that divine intelligence which created the universe, including man, a wholly spiritual creation. This Mind governs the universe. It's the power that holds sun and stars in their tracks and the earth in its orbit. It gave Jesus the power he used to move a ship instantly across a sea and roll away the stone from his tomb. Divine Mind is the only Mind that actually exists. As we read of God in the book of Job, "He is in one mind, and who can turn him?" (Job 23:13)

To live the "divine adventure" daily, a great deal is required in willingness to grow spiritually and scientifically and to pray humbly to God to reveal Himself to us, even if His nature and Being may prove to be contrary to our preconceived notions and educated beliefs. In today's scientific age, we have in Christian Science a scientific religion which can open up a life of divine adventure for anyone who will follow its Christly scientific teachings and rules, and so learn to know God as the one infinite governing intelligence.

The question whether we're living the divine adventure or the human misadventure largely depends on what we're permitting to influence us in our moment-to-moment living—divine Mind or mortal thinking.

Journey Under Divine Mind's Guidance

Let me tell you how I was helped to make what seemed an impossible journey across some 5,000 miles of ocean. I did this through an understanding of the power of divine Mind, and by disallowing mortal mind the power to spoil a progressive experience. When living in Australia, I came to realize how important it was for me to put my whole life under the guidance of divine Mind. And I wanted very much to study under a teacher of Christian Science living in San Francisco.

At the time World War 11 was not long over and no passenger ships had been put back on the Australia-United States run. But some planes were flying. So I booked passage with the airline, paid a deposit in local currency, and proceeded to sell our belongings. It was the intention that our family would proceed to Europe and eventually emigrate to the United States.

After doing all this, I found there was no dollar exchange between the two countries. Only in rare cases could dollars be granted such as for medical studies, or things to do with the government— certainly not for the purpose of studying Christian Science. And further, to obtain a visa I needed to show proof of support.

I'd been accepted for study by the teacher in San Francisco and had to keep a firm date. When told the bad news about the dollar exchange by the government bank official, I responded with a trustful, "God will surely provide another way then." So convinced was I of the rightness of my desire to know more about this Science that I felt no obstacle could deprive me of this progress. The teacher, who had lectured on Christian Science in Australia, seemed the right one for me. The bank official was so taken by my assurance and trust in God he requested information about my religion. I gave him a copy of *Science and Health*.

Now I must mention that, when our belongings were sold, I also sold my professional movie camera to a young moviemaker. Some days after my visit to the bank he telephoned me.

The conversation went something like this, "I hear you've booked passage for the U.S.A. How would you like to go there free?"

"Very much," I replied.

"How would you like to spend a day or so in Honolulu on your way over, and stop at a fine hotel— free? How would you like a car and chauffeur to drive you around there—free? And how would you like a substantial check in dollars when you get to San Francisco?"

By that time I'd had enough. "And what would you like for Christmas?" I asked him. But this was just how I came to study in San Francisco—with dollars to spare. The questions were all quite serious. My friend wanted to make a short travel film of a flight from Australia to San Francisco via Honolulu, and had discussed his project with the manager of the airline where I'd booked my passage. When he mentioned he'd purchased a movie camera from me it was suggested that I do the travel sequence in Honolulu and San Francisco with my own camera.

And so it happened. The film was made, using my family as the actors, and the camera was shipped back on the return plane.

Why had all this come about? Because at the crucial point when everything seemed to be going wrong, I'd refused to listen to the discouraging arguments of mortal mind. I'd listened only to the encouraging assurances of divine Mind—that God did love me and was too intelligent to deprive me of all I needed for my human career and spiritual growth.

This experience showed me how important it is to watch what's influencing one and to be sure it's divine Mind, God. Since then, I've proved the same point many times. Every one of us can live "Love's divine adventure" and find the All-in-all of good by resisting mortal mind's limiting suggestions and instead letting divine Mind govern our thought and therefore our experience.

Discovery of the Nothingness of Matter

Mrs. Eddy explored both the realm of divine Mind and the supposed realm of mortal mind, penetrating to mental regions hardly touched by men with the exception of Christ Jesus. Her revelation of the kingdom of Mind, God, can truly be called a "divine adventure." What Mrs. Eddy discovered in the realm of Mind, divine Love, of beauty, immortality, and grandeur, is now available for all to experience as a "divine adventure." She discovered a wholly spiritual universe, created by the divine Mind, and filled with perfect spiritual ideas of which men and women, understood in their true nature, are the highest.

Mrs. Eddy also discovered that what's termed matter is but a state of consciousness—mortal, human consciousness. This false consciousness projects its own images of what it calls matter, whether solid, liquid, or aeriform. But actually matter has neither substance nor permanence; it's no part of continuing reality.

Mrs. Eddy's discovery enabled her to give the world what she named "the scientific statement of being."

Let me read it: "There is no life, truth, intelligence, nor substance in matter. All is infinite Mind and its infinite manifestation, for God is All-in-all. Spirit is immortal Truth; matter is mortal error. Spirit is the real and eternal; matter is the unreal and temporal. Spirit is God, and man is His image and likeness. Therefore man is not material; he is spiritual." (Science and Health p.468)

Here we see that matter, while appearing to be solid substance to human consciousness, is but what we could call the thick end of mortal mind, and that mortal mind and matter are but different phases of mortal belief. Divine Mind is the one and only Mind; it's the Mind of man made in God's image and likeness. And it constitutes the only real enduring substance.

These spiritual truths revealed to Mrs. Eddy came from this same infinite divine intelligence, from God. They were the result of her prayerful searching of the Scriptures as well as of her spiritual receptivity and purity. She first glimpsed them when in a moment of great physical need they healed her, and in the years that followed they continued to unfold to her in their full meaning and implications. In 1875, nine years after her healing she published the first edition of *Science and Health*, the textbook of Christian Science.

Divine Mind Shows the Way to Physical Healing

Letting the divine Mind govern us, while eliminating mortal mind, not only can bring light and hope and the certainty of good into our human experience. It will also help us understand another area of vital concern to us if we're to lead a life of adventure—I refer to our health, our freedom from sickness.

The truths in "the scientific statement of being" I've just quoted, when allowed to influence and govern us, can raise us into an ever-higher concept and experience of health. They also make us less and less vulnerable to mortal mind's suggestions of disease.

On the other hand, seeking health through material remedies, drugs, makes us increasingly vulnerable to influences affecting one's health adversely. This adverse influence is described in an article written by a prominent doctor, Robert W. Shepherd, resident psychiatrist at Douglas Hospital, Montreal, Canada.

He writes: "Perhaps we don't realize the damage we've done in conditioning people to think sick. In an attempt to eliminate disease, we have created disease. Every day the news media, the medical profession, health societies, insurance companies, drug companies, and a host of others hammer home the same basic message: Be careful of your health. All this and more we do in the name of preventative medicine. The trends are clear and the results disastrous. In little more than one generation we have converted ourselves from a rugged self-reliant people into a group of tense, anxious neurotics." (National Inquirer, 2nd July, 1971, CA)

Doctor Shepherd finishes his article like this: "We should not underestimate the effects of thinking sick, nor lose time in correcting it. We simply need a total change in our approach to health care. Above all, we need to re-establish the sense of personal responsibility for personal health. For health is a highly personal thing,—God-given, not man-made. Health is an attitude of mind, a quality of Spirit."

Isn't Dr. Shepherd getting pretty close to Mrs. Eddy's position when he says that "health is God-given, not man-made;" that "health is an attitude of mind, a quality of Spirit." Yes, it is indeed our personal responsibility to see to it that divine Mind, not the human mind, is what influences us.

I remember, too, a woman speaking in a Christian Science Wednesday evening testimonial meeting. She related how a Los Angeles heart specialist whom she had consulted had said to her; "Madam, a heart is just a big muscle. There is nothing much to go wrong with it. A heart never kills a man, but men kill their hearts." She took his advice. As she gained an understanding of her true spiritual nature as the child of God, her character changed for the better and at the same time she was healed of her heart ailment.

Doctors such as these two from Montreal and Los Angeles are realizing that warning people against disease, describing symptoms, pushing drugs to heal, hasn't elevated mankind. It has, as Doctor Shepherd says, "converted rugged, self-reliant people into . . . tense, anxious neurotics."

As shown in the woman's healing of heart disease, the cardinal point in metaphysical healing is not the restoring of health to a physical body, but rather the healing of undesirable character traits and attitudes. Such healing can have a very wide range. It may mean overcoming a tendency to be hateful, envious, self-righteous or express any other form of self-love. Again, it may mean dispelling the belief that life is material which leads to a false sense of self and the attempt to heal matter with matter.

Christian Science turns men's thought away from dependence on material remedies. It releases mankind from the bondage of sickness through an understanding of God, Mind, and shows how to silence the suggestions of so-called mortal mind.

Understanding of the Christ Overcomes Opposition

However, spiritual healing, although practiced by Jesus, still receives much opposition, when practiced in Christian Science today.

Mrs. Eddy writes of this continuing opposition: "The law of the divine Mind must end human bondage, or mortals will continue unaware of man's inalienable rights and in subjection to hopeless slavery because some public teachers permit an ignorance of divine power,—an ignorance that is the foundation of continued bondage and of human suffering." (Science and Health p.227)

The misunderstanding of divine healing today is mostly due to a misunderstanding of the nature of the Christ. Many people still fail to understand the Christ-power to heal, because they identify the Christ solely with Jesus. But the Christ, the nature of God, the true idea of God and of man made spiritually in God's likeness—this Christ isn't limited to any single individual. Jesus assured his disciples that they and all who follow him would have the same power to heal. All could express the Christ, Truth, and the liberating power of this Truth.

Paul, who wasn't a personal follower or disciple of Jesus, understood the Christ and demonstrated his understanding in healing. He even raised a young man who'd fallen out of an upper story window from what was pronounced death. The author of the epistle to the Hebrews puts it in these words: "So Christ was once offered to bear the sins of many; and unto them that look for him shall he appear the second time without sin unto salvation." (Hebrews 9:28)

The Christ has already appeared again, and this time without a fleshly form, but rather as eternal Science. This Science of the Christ enables all to express, to respond to, that Mind, divine Mind, which was also in Christ Jesus.

For all those Christians who have in vain looked for Jesus to reappear on earth, Christian Science is indeed the Comforter, promised by Jesus. But this Comforter isn't to be understood until men's hearts are made ready for it—until the human mind, through humility, is willing to abandon its belief in the reality of sin, sickness and death, things healed by Jesus.

Mind Heals Sickness Caused by Mortal Mind

Like Paul, we too can understand the Christ and follow Jesus in his demonstration of healing and his dominion over every adverse condition. Jesus made possible, by his example, the highest type of adventure and showed the result of being constantly influenced by the divine Mind. Jesus demonstrated the Christly man wholly governed by God, and what such a man is capable of achieving. He was the Exemplar, the Way-shower who revealed the kingdom, the rule, of God in its eternal glory. We may not be able at first to do all the things Jesus did; but we can patiently and persistently begin to demonstrate the power of divine Mind to make our lives a "divine adventure."

Some years ago I proved in my own experience the healing power of the Christ and learned that health is a condition of divine Mind, while sickness is no more than a lying suggestion of mortal mind.

During an epidemic I found myself in a sanatorium suffering from an especially severe type of influenza. This illness came at a time I had listened to mortal mind's suggestions of frustration and despondency. And as I lay there, I heard mortal mind in consciousness saying, "Termination, termination."

That did it. Up until then I'd hardly been able to pray for myself as we're taught to do in Christian Science and had relied wholly on a Christian Science practitioner to help me. But now I was roused to do my part. I vigorously joined the practitioner in resisting mortal mind's suggestions and claimed the presence and allness of God, good.

My mental and spiritual resolve was accompanied by appropriate action. I managed to telephone friends from my bedside and asked them to come and help me to walk out of the sanatorium and put me on a plane home. I regained more and more control of my thinking as I shut out mortal mind's suggestions and let the divine Mind take over. I knew I was winning.

From that moment things got better. I managed to dress. Then the friends came and supported me physically and mentally to the plane. By the time I reached home, I no longer felt the need to lie down. I was able to eat. As I said to a friend who telephoned, I could see the end of the tunnel. The battle was soon won. In a few days I was well.

Although the struggle had been rough, as it sometimes is in such cases, I rejoiced that I had witnessed a victory over false beliefs, defeated mortal mind, and had proved the healing power of the divine Mind. I had even in this trying experience seen "Love's divine adventure" in spiritual healing.

Divine Mind Gives Insights into the Future

We've seen the importance of distinguishing between divine Mind and human or mortal mind if we're to have a life of high adventure. And we've seen how an understanding of divine Mind can ensure us the good health necessary for such a life. Now let's look at another area in which mortal thinking would lead us into misadventure while divine Mind will direct us aright. I refer to our expectations of the future.

As I've shown you, Christian Science reveals the glories of divine Mind and its healing and saving effect in the lives of humans. But it also thoroughly exposes the workings of evil through the so-called mortal mind. So let's first look at how mortal mind would mislead us as to our expectations.

Mrs. Eddy devotes an important chapter of *Science and Health* specifically to the unmasking of evil. She shows the basis of crime to be mental and that the supposed mortal, human mind—the imaginary opposite of divine Mind—is the evil influence causing all crime, misadventure and disease.

This perception prompted her to give a highly significant warning to all members of the Church she founded, the *Church of Christ, Scientist.* In her *Church Manual,* page 40, she writes: "The members of his Church should daily watch and pray to be delivered from all evil, from prophesying, judging, condemning, counseling, influencing or being influenced erroneously." Everyone, whether a member of this Church or not, who wishes to protect his future, does well to heed this warning.

Let me illustrate through an experience I had while in the Orient years ago.

The scene was a prisoner-of-war farm. Armed guards kept watch over the men digging hard, dry earth under a scorching sun. Their thoughts ranged from despair to violent revenge. I'd been appointed overseer of the group by our captors.

This particular day one of the guards, a quiet, kindly man who usually moved among the men unarmed, ordered me to come with him and interpret something he wanted to tell a prisoner. On reaching the man, who worked away from the others in a secluded spot, I was told to tell him that if he persisted in his bad thoughts he would be severely punished. The guard then quietly turned on his heels and went away.

Filled with curiosity, I inquired of my fellow-prisoner the meaning of all this. He admitted he'd often thought that, if one of those guards would ever come near and be alone with him, he'd bash his head in with his shovel. So violent was the suggestion of hatred and vengefulness he'd accepted from mortal mind, the guard had sensed the thoughts and intentions of the prisoner.

If the guard had been a less kindly man, the prisoner's thoughts might have landed him in severe punishment. We can't afford to let mortal mind map out our future for us.

Letting Divine Mind Determine our Future

The guard discerned his prisoner's thoughts in a clairvoyant way, by means of a type of mind reading which I found wasn't uncommon in the East. People there appear in many ways to have developed a keen sense for discerning insincerity, dishonesty, as well as danger.

Jesus also read the thoughts of those around him, of the disciples and of those he healed. But Mrs. Eddy writes of him: "Our Master read mortal mind on a scientific basis, that of the omnipresence of Mind." and further on, "Jesus could injure no one by his Mind-reading. The effect of his Mind was always to heal and to save, and this is the only genuine Science of reading mortal mind." (Science and Health p.94)

Many of the prophets of old foretold events of universal import. Isaiah prophesied that a virgin would bring forth a son whose name would be called Immanuel -which means "God with us." Micah prophesied that the child would be born in the town of Bethlehem. John the Baptist also foretold the coming of Christ Jesus. These Biblical prophecies are found in the Old and New Testaments.

Jesus, too, foretold great events. As recorded by Luke, he said: "There shall be signs in the sun, and in the moon, ... and upon the earth distress of nations, with perplexity; ... men's hearts failing them for fear, and for looking after those things which are coming on the earth: ... And when these things begin to come to pass, then look up, and lift up your heads; for your redemption draweth nigh." (Luke 21:25) Jesus also foretold the coming of a Comforter who would lead men into all truth.

In this the twentieth century, in spite of its turmoil, men can indeed lift up their heads, for their universal redemption from want and woe, sickness, sin, and death has come. The Christ, Truth, is here in all its fullness, healing and setting free. Instead of believing themselves to be poor physical mortals, the children of this glorious age of "Love's divine adventure" can learn to see themselves as spiritual ideas of divine Mind, the beloved children of God.

Mrs. Eddy at all times based her expectations for the future on intuitions from divine Mind and foretold great possibilities for this present century. She writes: "If the lives of Christian Scientists attest their fidelity to Truth, I predict that in the twentieth century every Christian church in our land, and a few in far-off lands, will approximate the understanding of Christian Science sufficiently to heal the sick in his name." (Pulpit and Press, page 22)

And healing the sick, though highly important in Christian Science, is but a first step. It arouses men to listen for the instruction and guidance of divine Mind in all areas, to find the liberating Truth that will heal all evil—war, poverty, unstable homes, and that great evil of our times, racism in all its guises, race hate, race fear, race conflict.

Of this high spiritual adventure Mrs. Eddy records her lively expectancy in these words, which surely apply directly to the efforts of all Christian churches to find a common ground for Christian fellowship:

"When the doctrinal barriers between the churches are broken, and the bonds of peace are cemented by spiritual understanding and Love, there will be unity of spirit, and the healing power of Christ will prevail. Then shall Zion have put on her most beautiful garments, and her waste places budded and blossomed as the rose." (Pulpit and Press, page 22). There, indeed, is a future of high adventure.

An Adventure for All of Us

And now, in conclusion, picture with me if you will, this glorious possibility—all Christendom, all Christian churches, responding to the Christ, Truth, healing sickness, sin, and all forms of evil in the way Jesus did, fulfilling his command, "Heal the sick, cleanse the lepers, raise the dead, cast out devils. (Matthew 10:8)

Picture, too, a society where spiritual understanding and love—governed and directed by the one infinite Mind—have replaced hatred, racial and otherwise, where peace prevails and war is outlawed, where the waste places of slums, pollution and blight are transformed into places of beauty.

This picture is a present possibility. The vision we behold we can achieve, and every one of us can experience a new and more beautiful world in this age through scientifically living "Love's divine adventure to be All-in-all."

INTRODUCING GLEN C. LIVEZEY

Glen Livezey, born into a Quaker family, grew up on a farm in a small town in Ohio. The male graduates in his town's high school were given their diplomas early so they could join the war effort. However, as this was towards the end of the Second World War, Glen's teenage service in the U.S. Coast Guard took place on American soil on the East Coast.

That generation's sense of duty extended well beyond the war years as they looked for work— not necessarily meaningful work—any legitimate undertaking to support their growing families. Glen told of carrying a television set from door-to-door to find someone who would try it out for a month, in the hope of making a sale. He adopted the same method when offering his services free for a whole month to an advertising agency. They liked his work and hired him. Glen eventually became an account executive at that agency.

Then, a life-changing event took Glen into a different world of endeavor and ideas. For a couple of years, he and another young man formed and operated a business called, "Ideation" which helped other businesses to think through and solve their problems. This was in effect a "think tank." Many copyrights were gained by companies that incorporated the new solutions and ideas the young men presented.

Glen next entered a new arena of advertising, that of working for the Christian Science Monitor as National Advertising Manager. He transitioned from there into the public practice of Christian Science healing and then onto the lecture platform and circuit as a member of the Christian Science Board of Lectureship. His lecturing schedule extended across the United States (sometimes into high-security prisons), then to Canada and to Europe.

In his first lecture, "Let Your Basis be Love," Glen speaks of finding a whole new basis for his life. He had glimpsed the reality of being and viewed life from a mountaintop or spiritual perspective. But more than that view is required as he found out. One might begin a baseball game at home plate but the bases still need to be run. We all have to prove the spiritual reality.

So, in his second lecture, "Who Do You Think You Are?" he shows the necessity for this spiritual journey as he relates his personal transformation and shows how it brought physical healing from a crippling condition. Glen found a higher sense of identity for himself, which enabled him to lift and heal other lives. More about his journey can be found in the book, *Quiet Answers*.

Glen did wonderful healing work and today, many years after his passing, some of those healings are still recounted to me. He walked out of so many of the limitations of material life and living by taking the spiritual pathway to freedom.

A.W.L.

LET YOUR BASIS BE LOVE

Let Your Basis be Love

Glen C. Livezey, C.S.

Early one morning a man I know went to his church. As he started to unlock the door, he noticed the lock had been jimmied. He rushed inside and found another door whose lock had been cut away. On the secretary's desk he found amplifiers, microphones, typewriters—everything portable and valuable.

On top of the pile was this note:

Dear Sir,

I've broken into your church. I was going to rob you blind, but I couldn't. I'm a teenager and a boy. I hate myself, but I wish I could be a square. I can't go straight ... I don't know why. I don't believe in God. How can I? He has never done anything for me. Still I can't take away from your faith by wrecking up your church. I wish I had faith. I'm with my friend now. We were the ones that broke into the Central School. I must go now, but I hope you can help people who haven't gotten to the point I have.

Keep cool.

Love

(I wish I could in my heart)

And his friend had scribbled what, in effect, said, "Me, too."

These boys broke into the church intending to destroy and rob. They even admitted breaking into the Central School. Then how can we account for the fact they didn't go ahead in this case? And why did they bother to write the note? Didn't that take time—time that increased the possibility of their getting caught? Possibly the answer lies in how they closed that note. "Love (I wish I could in my heart}."

Could it be that these two boys felt the love the members held for their church—felt it enough to want to share in it? There's no way of knowing for sure. The boys' identities have never been learned. But I can tell you this, that the members surely felt divine Love protected both their church and those boys that night.

Tonight we're going to discuss the kind of love held by those members for their church—the love that apparently influenced both boys—and its source, *divine* Love. We'll discuss how selecting *divine* Love as the basis of life will influence our experience, too.

Love's Qualities Seen

To explore divine Love as the basis of life, we find it's not so much in the words we use but in what's behind the words. For instance, it'd be difficult for most of us here to describe in words the feeling of joy, of inner exuberance, we have when we've really accomplished something worthwhile. We can say it's a "good feeling," but that doesn't quite do it. It doesn't quite touch the profound sense of inner peace we feel ... the inner warmth. It has to be felt. To bring out the feeling we're discussing, I'd like to "point at" some of the qualities divine Love includes.

First of all tenderness. As tender as you very well may feel toward those boys who broke into that church. That gentle warmth of compassion, this is the feeling I'm talking about. And you can see it's not just an intellectual exercise. It's warmer – fuller—and goes deeper than any group of words. It's an outpouring of warmth. And it's this warmth you feel.

And still, divine Love is more than tenderness.

Love brings peace. The absolute quiet of true peace—nothing unsteady or threatening. The kind of peace we feel, rather than just say.

For example, how many of you have driven through the mountains and seen the signs that say, "Scenic Vista Ahead"? Then, as you leave the car, you leave the hustle and bustle of the trip behind.

Pine needles carpet the ground muffling every step you take. A sharp cry of a blue jay accentuates the stillness. Then you walk to the edge. It's as if every feeling of quiet you've ever felt were magnified a hundred times.

Stillness, immense peace permeates the whole scene. It's this immensity, this feeling, that comes even before the words that may describe it. It's basically the fullest appreciation you hold of your experience. It's this peace you feel—and still divine Love is more.

Love is Infinite

Now picture yourself at home reading a newspaper. On page one there's a picture, let's say, of a Chinese peasant smilingly offering a gift to a small child. On page three, another picture. This one lets us see the radiant joy of an African woman as she receives, say, an award.

As you leaf through other pages, you see other pictures from all over the world. It's evident the joy you saw expressed in China wasn't confined to China. You saw it expressed in the smile of the African woman and in some of the other pictures, too.

Joy just isn't confined to geography or persons because the exhilaration called "joy" is a quality of divine Love. There's no such thing as a two-by-four piece of joy. There's no edge or limit to joy. It's boundless. Not more here than there, but everywhere. Like the immensity of the Scenic Vista, the beauty nature holds is everywhere. So the feeling of tenderness brought out by those troubled boys is available everywhere.

Now, let's put these qualities together. Take the feeling of tenderness we feel and expand it and expand it again. Yet God's divine Love is still more. And the feeling of immensity ... the immense sense of peace we feel. Expand that and expand it again. Yet divine Love is still more. And the joy expressed in those faces from all over the world we saw in our newspaper. Take that joy and expand it, and yet divine Love is still more. Because divine Love isn't bound by anything. It's everywhere. It's infinite. Then we see we're not just talking about love—but about divine Love, a Love that's God Himself. And a God that is Love.

Love Is Power

I had an experience with a garage mechanic which brings out the infinite nature and power of divine Love. I'd taken my car to have a minor adjustment. The mechanic told me to come back in an hour to pick it up. I did. The car hadn't been touched. I went back a second time and still no car. I was a bit irritated. Well, maybe more than a bit! I called the mechanic's boss and registered my complaint—and my irritation, too.

Now, about this time, I also started to recognize I hadn't been loving at all in my attitude. Regardless of the apparent inconvenience, I couldn't find any real peace until I got my thinking straight. So I put aside the irritation and inconvenience and thought of all the examples of divine Love I could, until I began to feel God's boundless love flooding my consciousness. In a way, I'd been praying, and I began to feel the effect of my prayer.

In this much more enlightened frame of thinking, I went back to pick up my car. Apparently the mechanic's boss had relayed my remarks to him. As I came into the station, the mechanic came bursting out through the door. His face was livid with rage. He reached out to grab me by the collar. His fist was clenched. And he started to swing! But he stopped right in midair. His expression changed. His arms dropped to his sides and he turned and went back into the filling station. I can't tell you the gratitude that welled up in me as I recognized the Love I'd been praying to. Why, the power of this Love had extended and included him.

He came out a few minutes later smiling— and my car was now adjusted. He apparently had no recall of his former anger at all. Courtesy, even friendliness, had replaced his anger. You see as I related to divine Love as God, the power of God's love was reflected in my experience.

This discovery is important. As we perceive that divine Love is actually God, we find ourselves bringing forth tenderness, love, compassion, and goodness in our lives. But we're also aligning with all the good, all the joy there is. One reference that has been helpful to me in this recognition is from *Science and Health with Key to the Scriptures*, by

Mary Baker Eddy, the Discoverer of Christian Science. It reads, " 'God is Love.' More than this we cannot ask, higher we cannot look, farther we cannot go." [1]

Think of that! Why, if each of us would relate to Love as God, think how difficult—downright impossible—it would be for any one of us to have an argument with anyone. In infinite Love there just isn't room for irritation. Love precludes it. The power of Love is infinite.

Dropping False Basis of Thought

With Love as our God—as our basis for thinking and action—our lives, yours and mine, will be directly affected. For whatever is unlike our God—everything unlovely—will no longer have a place in our lives.

A friend of mine had an experience that brings this out. She always had a strong fear, even resentment, of the street gangs that weren't far from her home—not far enough, if you'd asked her! This antagonistic view caused her much anxiety.

A friend of hers, who lived in this street gang area, mentioned she couldn't carry much money because of the frequent robberies. Well! When my friend heard that, her self-righteous anger boiled over at this intrusion upon personal freedom. When my friend was all through steaming and fuming, her friend quietly said all she felt was compassion for these youths. Not to excuse their acts so much as to recognize why these young people did what they did, she went on to explain they had almost no parental guidance. They were often turned into the streets to fend for themselves when they were just old enough to walk. They didn't know anything other than such gang tactics. They just didn't know a different way.

Well, my friend thought about it. As a Christian Scientist, she realized that human compassion, in itself, wasn't enough. She had to go further. She also saw her unloving, brittle viewpoint had been shutting off any real help she could ever have brought to these youths. So, in renewed humility she turned to divine Love to correct her thinking. She prayed to see them in a new light. She began to view them from the basis of divine Love, itself. Right where destruction and robbery seemed to predominate, she knew Love was the only presence. She saw, from this basis of Love, man as God created him. Spiritual. Free. Intelligent. Not ghetto-bred, never criminally inclined at all. But unburdened, beloved, forever blessed.

The Love she was acknowledging shone right through her in practical ways . . . dissolving her fears, allowing fresh new ideas to bring solutions to the ghetto, by becoming active in ghetto politics, and by supporting and promoting a day-care and educational center. Prejudice was replaced by Love-impelled action that has blessed not only her, but also the very areas and people she once so feared.

How many of us have ever felt—and wanted to keep—the angry, bitter feelings that well up within us? Those inflexible false prejudices that limit our true appreciation of the good around us? As we relate to divine Love as our premise, false bases for living fade and are dissolved in Love's acknowledged presence.

Some Prejudices Dissolved

I don't know about you, but for a long time I had the general impression that prejudice pretty much referred to racial issues. But prejudice refers to any kind of prejudgment. Can't we limit or obstruct our gentleness, our joy, and peace, if we wrongly prejudge ourselves and others? We do this when we hold false or unwarranted views of who and what we are.

Those boys who intended to rob that church surely held false, downright prejudiced views of themselves. They judged or evaluated themselves as limited mortals. Remember, their letter said, "I hate myself -I can't go straight, 1 don't know why." Such personal prejudices against ourselves obscure God's infinite presence from our lives, just as those boys' prejudice had been doing to them.

Such prejudices or prejudgments accepted for ourselves may extend to other people in our lives. For instance, I once held a strong bias against women. As a male, I felt I couldn't be told anything of moment or value by a woman. There's a prejudice for you! You can imagine the peace that one gave me! And on top of that, as you know, Mary Baker Eddy founded Christian Science. Since she was a woman—well, you can see the problem I had.

Of course, my male prejudice didn't start with Mrs. Eddy. Apparently, it stemmed from my acceptance of the generally held belief of male superiority. And this, in turn, was rooted in the false premise of a "partial" God—a God that would give one more good than another. As long as I held to the belief of a God who played favorites, I was prejudicing my whole view of man—man in the image of God, absolute, spiritual Love.

I had another bias that stood in my way of really feeling the peace and gentleness of Love. It was reluctance to read the Bible. With pride, I steered away from the Bible since I just knew I was never going to be a churchgoer, let alone join a church. And these prejudiced views against the Scriptures were stubbornly held to by me as what really was important. I was shutting out Love. My introduction to Christian Science changed that. It brought a quick healing—in fact, overnight—of a bad back condition that was all but crippling me. Well, I was grateful for that healing, honestly grateful. I had to find out what had healed me.

Since I recognized Christian Science is based directly on the Scriptures, respect, then affection, for the Bible and a real sense of the Bible's worth began to dawn on me. For a start I found a rich store of history as well as poetry and prose, enrichments my former prejudice had denied me.

Then, as I began to accept Love as my premise, I began to notice something else. I saw that divine Love—the same Love I was relating to—was the premise of the entire Bible. Moses listened to it. The prophets listened to it. And Jesus listened to it, too. Why, I could suddenly see divine Love shining right through his healings. You can see I was awakening to a new dimension of the Bible—the spiritual.

My prejudice had been so pronounced it had obscured the very essence of the Bible from me. I suddenly felt the timeless nature of the Christ, Truth, and understood better what Jesus had meant when he described his healing mission as God-ordained and God-directed. I realized he was referring to this Christly nature when he said, "I and my Father are one." [2] One with God, Love. And also, "As I hear, I judge: and my judgment is just; because I seek not mine own will, but the will of the Father which hath sent me." [3]

What can God, the Father, be but Love? And Love wouldn't prejudice. Love is just.

Well, with this new and much deeper sense of the Bible, I began to appreciate *Science and Health* with its Key to the Scriptures. *Science and Health* had come out and openly challenged the orthodox theology of that day and its traditional interpretation of the Bible. My growing respect began to extend to its author, Mrs. Eddy. And more of my male-chauvinist prejudices began to melt. I realized that in the year 1875 when *Science and Health* was first published, women were accorded no better than a second-class citizenship. Here was a woman with what had to be some of the greatest courage I'd ever even considered.

Imagine presenting a book like *Science and Health* to the world, a world so set in its ways, a world filled with prejudice and resistance—even open attacks on anything new, let alone, radical. I began to glimpse the love Mrs. Eddy must have felt for this world, and my own petty prejudices dissolved. It took fearless love, real courage, to bring out this book with its revolutionary premise—that God, Spirit, is All. Infinite. And wholly good. That His creation, man, is like unto Himself—perfect, spiritual, and whole. And, therefore, that evil and the limitations of matter have no part in Love's creation.

Mistaken Identity the Basis of Prejudice

There's no reason for any of us to accept prejudice against our true selves as a basis for identity. It would be a mistake to think that prejudice could provide us with an identity. If we did, that's just what we'd have—a case of mistaken identity.

For isn't mistaken identity the basis of all prejudice? Have you even been mistaken as someone else by a stranger? That happened to me one time in downtown Boston. This exuberant young man came running up to me. Pumping my hand, he exclaimed, "Hello, George!" Now, my name's not George. But when I told him this helpful bit of information, he was still shaking his head at how much I looked like his friend "George."

Prejudice is like this. It's a case of mistaken identity because it's built on a false basis. I wasn't George. But even when this man was told I wasn't, he held on to his mistake. In other words, it's sometimes easy for us to expose a false premise. I wasn't George. But it sometimes takes some real digging to root out our old way of thinking.

No matter how difficult it may seem to be to shake false bases of identity, we'll never know the real man until we do. And where does this uncovering of false premises and proper identification go on? Right where it did with George's friend. In his own thinking. Right in his consciousness. And that's just where I had to correct my male prejudice. Right in my thinking where, if left alone, it would continue to distort and confuse.

Each one of us can uncover and deny these errors of judgment against ourselves and others and defeat their insistent holds. As we've seen, no matter what guise these prejudices may appear in, they'll conceal the inherent good, success, and joy of our lives.

To dissolve these prejudices, we need to firmly feel our true basis in Love. Then, from this basis, we need to see we can only be what God has made us. Since God is infinite, there isn't anything outside His creation. The teachings of Christian Science make clear that we must expose and dismiss everything from our thinking that infringes on our real nature in God's image.

As we affirm the Truth, the false expression which Mrs. Eddy calls "mortal man" dissolves like the shadows before the dawn. No matter how grotesque the shadows are, the dawn melts them away. And in the same way we increasingly see ourselves as God-created. We're not Spirit's opposite, matter, or Love's opposite, a sinner. We're the expression of God, inseparable from Him. Spiritual. Free.

Just think of our lives without prejudice! Free from false judgments of any sort. Our lives expressed out from the basis of infinite Love, itself. Think what this means ... no depreciating self-evaluations. In the absolute blessing of infinite Love, there's just no room for anything unworthy of Love—no place for self-condemnation. In the fulfilling presence of absolute Love there's no empty feeling of limitation or inadequacy. There's no lack of any spiritual good—only the forever expanding recognition of all good. In infinite Love there's no gnawing judgment of guilt or fear. There's only the wholeness, the purity of Love to know right now, in all directions, forever. Our lives, yours and mine, free of every false evaluation, false judgment, every false bias. Expressed right from the basis of all-blessing, divine Love. Pure, uncontaminated.

Right here and now as we base our lives in God as absolute Love, we abandon the prejudices of materiality. Instead, we find more joy, peace, gentleness in our lives. We find them shining through us, revealing and supporting all the good around us . . . all that's good in our lives.

Love's Control Lifts Us

Love's control lifts our lives into new activity and purpose. Perhaps you've never considered Love's control. Perhaps you've always thought of control as domination, even where love is supposed to be, such as in marriage or between parent and child.

In consideration of Love's control, let's return to that episode with the mechanic. Why he hadn't hit me offers us an important point. Since I was feeling a sense of God's love as unselfed and universal, there wasn't any place for hate. The darkest night can't put out the glow of Love. Anger or hate can't penetrate the infinite presence of Love. Mrs. Eddy writes in *Science and Health*, "Science shows appearances often to be erroneous, and corrects these errors by the simple rule that the greater controls the lesser." The greater controls the lesser. Love's control stems from this fact. Consider this thought. You've never seen a shaft of darkness enter a lighted room. Why not? Because light is the greater idea, greater than the absence of light called darkness. No wonder the light always wins out!

As I stand here and close my fist and peek inside, I see some darkness. And it sure seems present. You might want to check inside your fist to see if you have some, too. Now, let's open our hands and find nothing at all (unless, perhaps, some of you have a little mound of dark). No? Because the light was greater all along. If you opened your hand one million times, there wouldn't be even one time when the light didn't eclipse the absence of itself, called darkness. Think of that, not once! Light never fails.

In the physical realm light always controls the absence of itself, called darkness. So in the spiritual realm, divine Love precludes the lack of itself—hate, impurity, or fear. The greater controls the lesser, every time.

Think back to the young men who broke into the church. It was their higher sense of love that dissolved the lesser idea of vandalism and burglary. The prejudiced view held by my friend for the ghetto gangs was dissolved in a scientific understanding of divine Love. Her reflection of God as Love has enabled her to be of service in the very neighborhood she feared. In the same way, orderliness destroys the absence of itself, disorder, every time. Intelligence destroys the absence of itself, stupidity, every time. Joy, the absence of itself, sadness, every time.

How can we bring out more of these greater ideas? How can we bring out more of this good which is the divine substance of Love in our lives? It's simple—so simple a bustling world would rush right by it. We have to relate to God, divine Love, as All-in-all, as absolute, basic Being. As we do acknowledge this basis for our thinking and action, Love asserts the fact of its allness and controls all, dissolving all unlike itself. Love brings the flow of tenderness, the serenity of true inner peace, the warmth and beauty of gentleness. Divine Love is greater than everything else.

We need this conviction of knowing—and knowing we know—that God, good, is in control. And He is, every time. There have been many times when I'd close my fist and open it to the light, time after time, to build my conviction that the greater *always* controls the lesser. Always. When we see this fact, as we recognize the inevitability of this law, we glimpse the inevitability of God's control. The greater controls the lesser, every time.

Acknowledgment Brings Healing

I had an experience that proves the importance of this acknowledgment of divine Love. My very life was being threatened. One day I noticed my throat was sore. There was a large, swollen protrusion. A year or so earlier I had had a similar problem. At that time a ruptured tumor was removed surgically.

107

And here it was again, more pronounced than before. When I'd had the operation, I wasn't studying Christian Science. But now I was, so I sought the help of an experienced Christian Scientist.

I was so choked with fright, I almost couldn't talk at times. Yet I'd already seen enough of the power of prayer in my experience to know this was the kind of treatment I wanted. At first, all I could think about was my problem and its ominous appearance. The discomfort didn't help much either. I found I was relating everything I was doing on the basis of my problem. I wouldn't do this or that because of how I felt.

My problem had become my basis of living. The fear of it colored, actually prejudiced, everything I was doing. The help of the experienced Christian Scientist was, well, tremendous. One citation she gave me to study is from *Science and Health*. It reads: "Self-love is more opaque than a solid body. In patient obedience to a patient God, let us labor to dissolve with the universal solvent of Love the adamant of error,—self-will, self-justification, and self-love,—which wars against spirituality and is the law of sin and death." [5]

Well, this citation made me angry. I felt it was telling me I was self-willed, self-justifying, and self-loving. And then it hit me. I saw the Love in what she was sharing. I saw I'd been accepting a false basis of myself. I suddenly realized it was this false, prejudiced, and fear-filled basis that had to be dissolved. It wasn't really the tumor at all!

Well, I have to admit I was still reluctant to let go of all my prejudgment of myself as a fearful, material mortal all at once. But I did see some prejudices against myself begin to dissolve. Egotism or self-importance, for one. And the fear lessened. I quit checking on the condition all the time. More and more I changed my thinking and acknowledged Spirit instead of matter to be my basis. I began to find the harmony of God as divine Love, greater than everything else expressed in my experience. I began to see that God was right where the discordant condition tried to say it was. Now, this was prayer in its highest form—the acknowledgment of God's allness and man's present spiritual perfection as God's child.

It didn't happen all at once. There were days of discouragement. But I held on. I kept praying in this way. The infinitude and power of divine Love began to take hold in my life. The fear left. My whole concern now was one of knowing more of my divine basis, Love. I studied the Bible and the Christian Science textbook daily to support my growing awareness of my true spiritual nature. I mentally prayed that I couldn't be now and never was matter based at all. That God had created me, and I could have no qualities but those God had for me. I didn't look to what the physical evidence was saying at all.

A month or so after the problem began, while I was shaving, I happened to glance at my throat. It was no longer swollen or sore. Health had replaced disease. Wholeness replaced the distortion and pain. I was healed. The absolute control of infinite Love had operated in my life—and completely changed my life. For several years now I've been happily working in the full-time public practice of Christian Science.

As each of us acknowledges God, divine Love, as the basic premise of our thinking, as the greater basis for our actions, we find healing and love expressed in our lives. This is the activity of the Christ, Truth. Self expressed. Self enforced. This Christ-power dissolves all unlike itself. It is God's love expressing itself in human experience. The greater controlling the lesser every time. This self-enforcing, spiritual activity is God's forever expressing the truth of His Allness. His infinitude.

The Christ, Truth, is the same power Jesus expressed without measure in his ministry. But it wasn't confined to him. Christ is the ideal Truth operative and available to all throughout all time. Jesus expressed this power more than all others, so much so that he was called "Jesus the Christ" and "Christ Jesus." It was this same power my friend employed when she was healed of the prejudice concerning those ghetto gangs.

This Christ-power, this truth, this love is here right now for you and me to live. As we honestly try to base our lives in God, divine Love, each of us can more and more experience its redemptive effect. The Christ-power brings forth vital, new experiences, fresh purpose, and healing.

Transforming Nature of Love

A woman I know experienced this exalting influence of the Christ, Truth, in her life. She had been plagued for some twenty years by a severe, cracking condition of her hands. She was a hairdresser, so you can imagine how difficult this situation was for her. She had to continually dip her hands in all kinds of lotions and rinses, and the like. The condition had become so aggravated she often couldn't do the simplest household job, let alone work at her profession. Fear became her motivation. She had seen doctor after doctor, and taken radium treatments from the last one.

She knew of Christian Science, and finally, in desperation, she called a Christian Science practitioner for help. She gave the practitioner almost no time to say anything beyond an occasional, "Oh," or "Yes, I see." However, as she told all the details, the practitioner held to what he knew was really true for her. He drew his conclusions from the basis of divine Love, not the material evidence that was being described as so distressing. He knew that in the truth of being, good was dominating. He mentally affirmed the fact that the goodness God expresses never held anything unlike Love. The infinite nature of divine Love wouldn't allow it.

Suddenly, in a trembling voice the woman said, "Why my hands, they're changing right before my eyes!" Then she hung up. When she called back later, she fully described the healing that occurred in about fifteen minutes while she sat, an amazed witness!

The Christ, Truth, had touched this woman's life. The transforming nature of God's love was glimpsed by her. She began to see she was whole in Love. Love, if faintly, had become her basis of thought. And the greater always controls the lesser. Love eclipsed the limiting physical condition and she realized her healing.

Not only was the physical healing permanent, but Love's self-enforcing goodness has been increasingly controlling this woman's whole life.

The Highest Vista

We talked earlier about the scenic vista. We're all at that mountaintop in reality now. Our lives express divine Love. Our whole experience relates to this exalted view of ourselves and others. From this high view we see unlimited man and an unobstructed universe. From this high place we see God as the only cause and our experience as the divine outcome of His nature.

And no matter how problems and lies of lack would try to obscure our high stand, spiritually we're at the mountaintop. And *everything* relates to where we are. Any limited recognition of our high place as Love's own doesn't change the fact of where we are spiritually. It would only try to obscure what's been for all time true about us. No matter how incessantly old conceptions try to hold us down, we're at the mountaintop of Spirit.

Divine Love transforms us as we give up our earthly, matter-bound prejudices for what God holds as true about us. It's the real being real, the spiritual being all.

I sometimes picture whatever would try to hide this reality as much like the storms that gather around a mountain peak. If you watched the storm—became entranced by its darkness and violence—you might lose sight momentarily that the peak itself is really unmoved. The storm never was a part of it at all. Just so, we're never really part of the lie that tries to obscure our view of where we stand. Our spiritual mountaintop can never be the mortal storm around it regardless of how severe that claim may be. We're impelled to be what God, Spirit, has made us. And we're absolutely unmovable in this spiritually right view of ourselves and man.

Our high view expands as we release everything that would dim it. As we see we're not in the storm at all. We then see we're not trying to get rid of this particular physical problem or that business situation. That's not the issue at all. What we're really about is being God's expression. We're acknowledging the Truth about us as wholly free from everything ungodlike. Expressed by God we can only be what He holds for us. His nature never included problems of lack or ill health, and ours can't either. In *Science and Health* we read, "God expresses in man the infinite idea forever developing itself, broadening and rising higher and higher from a boundless basis." [6]

As we glimpse our true standpoint at the mountaintop, nothing but an ever-clearer view of our whole nature can really fulfill. Suddenly our purpose shifts from trying to remake the storms of our lives to expressing our whole nature, which dissolves the storms in the recognition they never were ours or anyone's ... never touched us at all.

We're God's blessed work. His transforming nature never leaves us where we thought we were. It shows us more of our own divine nature in Him already at the mountaintop—and expresses us as this very love.

Right Identity Vital

No question about it. As we rely on Love as the spiritual scientific basis for our thinking and prayer, our lives will express more of divine Love. Gentleness, compassion, true quiet, inner peace, health, wholeness, joy. And as we increasingly acknowledge our true nature as Love's own, we express our spiritual identity. It's not something we merely hope for. Not something that some day may be true about us. But as we acknowledge the allness of divine Love, our spiritual identity is lived now.

1. Science and Health, p.6
2. John 10:30
3. John 5:30
4. Science and Health, p. 121
5. Ibid., p. 242
6. Ibid., p. 258

WHO DO YOU THINK YOU ARE?

Who Do You Think You Are?

Glen C. Livezey, C.S.

A man stood alone on a river bank. His thoughts were filled with fear—dark as the night closing in around him. He'd drawn apart from the group he was traveling with. He felt separated from everything.

He'd deceived his father. He'd cheated his brother. His own mother had connived with him in doing this. His brother's threats had driven him away from home and family. And after his years of exile and separation, his brother was after him with a band of men. Desperation nearly overwhelmed him.

I expect by now most of you recognize the Biblical character I'm talking about. Jacob was suddenly forced to face all his misdeeds. That dark night his burden of guilt was so strong that in his frenzy he literally rolled in the dust, wrestling with his tortured thoughts. So real seemed the self-condemnation, so acute was the fear, that the book of Genesis describes his struggle as if it were with another person. It reads, "There wrestled a man with him until the breaking of the day." [1]

The struggle was really with himself—with his own sense of right. His higher sense was trying to assert itself over his guilt and fear. The dawn referred to in the Bible passage *did* come. His higher sense did win out. It won to such a degree he was no longer even called by his old name "Jacob." From then on he was "Israel." He was a new man. His meeting with his brother was not only peaceful but gifts and warm expressions of brotherly love were exchanged. And his whole life after that was one of increasing fulfillment.

Though most of us aren't faced with a struggle comparable to Jacob's, many of us have felt a gnawing discontent with life. A sort of self-contradiction between what we're doing day after day and what we, back of it all, feel we really could be doing.

St. Paul writes, "We wrestle not against flesh and blood, but against principalities, against powers, against the rulers of the darkness of this world, . . . "[2] We're going to consider together how we can apply some spiritually scientific rules which will help us find that new man which is our better self, our true self.

A Glimpse of True Selfhood Brings Health

Do you remember the last time you didn't do the best you could? Maybe it was with a close friend, a neighbor, or a member of your family? Perhaps it was something you said you really wished you hadn't, back of it you really knew better. Wasn't that uneasiness you felt one "you," wrestling with another "you"?

Wasn't the British writer Thomas Carlyle directing us toward this self-contradiction when he wrote, "Man's unhappiness, ... comes of his greatness; it is because there is an Infinite in him, which with all his cunning he cannot quite bury under the Finite."[3] Yes, most of us have many struggles between the Jacob and Israel of us.

Take the experience of a man I know. He was in advertising. His career was blossoming. He had regular raises in pay and improvements in title and responsibility. He prided himself on being able to get along with clients.

Yet from time to time he had some anxious moments. Sometimes when he'd been caught by a client in a story of why this or that wasn't done, with sweating hands and brow he'd cover up. At times he felt forced to bend the truth—well, to lie, a white lie—for "business reasons." He felt stress in what he was doing. I know so much about this young man because I was that man.

I really didn't like to do what I was more and more being asked to do. I'd try to put down that nagging little voice of conscience by justifying myself. The more I felt that inner rebellion, the more I felt trapped by what I was doing.

The struggle, not too unlike Jacob's, put an increasing mental burden on me. So much so that my back, physically, began to hurt under the strain. One time, for example, it took me 20 minutes to walk just a block and a half from my office to my car. And for three years I went to one doctor after another trying to get relief.

The last constructed a brace for me. It fitted up under my shoulders and went down over my hips. I had to wear it, more and more—taking it off before I'd go to sleep and putting it on before I got up. I was also told I should have an operation.

During this time one of the people who called on me at my office began to leave copies of the daily newspaper she represented, The Christian Science Monitor. I'd wait 'til she was gone and drop them into the waste basket. This went on for a year, until finally I began to read that newspaper. There's a short article about God in every issue. I began to read that, too. Then as I'd go out in my job through airports and bus terminals other Christian Science literature—the weekly Christian Science Sentinel— would catch my eye. And now and then I'd pick up copies and read them, too. Well, one day my back seemed particularly bad.

When I got to my desk, I sat there holding on to some thoughts about God I'd just been reading. God as support—my support and everyone's. I suddenly felt compelled to take off the brace. I rode home that night in less discomfort with the brace off than I had coming in with it on. The next morning I woke up and didn't have any pain at all. It was a little like waking up from a bad dream—a dream I suddenly saw I didn't have to go along with anymore. It was as if I were Jacob. I'd awakened to find a new man—Israel.

Our True Selfhood Expresses Divine Spirit

What happened to bring this about? I'd made an important discovery. You may have noticed I didn't say I became a new man, but that I found a new man. I'd discovered what's really always there. The real you and the real me is healthy and whole and free all the time. Instead of having to go along with a burdened self, each of us is spiritually whole and free.

Mary Baker Eddy, the Discoverer and Founder of Christian Science, put it this way in her book *Science and Health with Key to the Scriptures*, "Science reveals the glorious possibilities of immortal man, forever unlimited by the mortal senses." [4] Doesn't this explain why I had a victory over my false sense of self? Because I awoke to see in some degree that man in reality is forever perfect, complete.

The apparent self-contradiction, then, is the struggle between the belief we're physical organisms of human or material origin and the fact we're wholly spiritual expressions of God Himself. Between material imperfection and spiritual wholeness. This is the battle Jacob, had—with his mortal, self-deceived nature and the real of him, the Israel of him—the true self Jacob never had, but Israel always expressed.

And in a measure this is just what I discovered. I'd glimpsed my true nature, my present spiritual identity in God, impelled by God. Not a big glimpse, but enough to displace some of my old thoughts of myself. As my old limited, burdened, matter-centered thinking was replaced by the real me, by the Israel-me, my spiritual selfhood expressed itself in my human experience. That's another way of saying I was healed.

The real of us, then, is our entity in God, the one, ever present Spirit. It's God's blessed work. This identity Christian Science teaches is therefore holy spiritual, the likeness of Spirit, God. Suddenly, I realized that God, Spirit, is the absolute all. Not a psychological safety valve for the convenience of my use or misuse, but the absolute basis of man, known spiritually. The real of you. The real of me. It was this that healed me, that wakened me to who I really am.

The Christ, Truth, of Spiritual Selfhood Displaces the Belief in Material Selfhood

One individual brought out, perhaps more than all others, this real of man, Jesus. He's someone I frankly didn't feel as relevant—he lived so long go. But with my study of Christian Science I began to appreciate the timeless nature of all he proved. Here, recorded in the Bible for us all to discover and follow is his living example of right identity—of recognizing "man's true selfhood in the Christ, the ideal of God, divine Truth. In fact, he identified so consistently with this ideal that he was known as "Christ Jesus" or "Jesus the Christ."

It's his example of living the Christ that Christian Scientists work to follow. He healed. He helped those about him. And he made it clear we could do the same. As we see man as God created him—as Jesus proved him—we find our own true selfhood in the Christ, too.

So it was with me. As I began to recognize myself as based in God, Spirit, I saw I'd no legitimate basis for believing I was material or matter-based. God couldn't express anything unlike His own nature. One statement I found particularly enlightening in this recognition is from *Science and Health*, "Spirit is God, and man is His image and likeness. Therefore man is not material; he is spiritual." [5] Not material, you see, but spiritual; not even a little material, but wholly spiritual. God is Spirit. Therefore I was spiritual. I saw I couldn't be spiritual and at the same time something unlike Spirit. I couldn't be both. That was the very conflict I was awakening from. That there were two of me.

As more and more I accepted God as ever-present Spirit and myself as His expression, I'd sit by the hour considering just how deeply this recognition affected every phase of my life. The way I felt about my home life, business, personal relations. I'd just sit there and revel in what this discovery meant. That now I could be me, *really*. Not a phony. Not someone else. Not what the ads or TV told me to be. But me right from God.

I began to understand how every one of us can express better health—like my healing when we wake up to our true selfhood in God. God, whose creation is spiritually perfect, because *He* is perfect. God, whose creation hasn't a vestige of matter or matter's elements of limitation and destructibility, of turmoil and frustration. Spirit, not matter, is the real of creation and of man.

Of course, the world would try to divert us from this discovery of our true selfhood by offering many alternatives to the spiritual. These diversions are all around us, and some of them offer well-meaning attempts to help. In my own case, the doctors I saw did their best, I'm certain. The brace I wore did alleviate the pain. But was that really what I needed? Wasn't my need deeper than backache? Wasn't it in the brittle self-justification and the worldly burden I thought I carried?

Wasn't it plain that my comfort could only come spiritually—when I unloaded my false sense of myself? As long as I dealt with the imperfect, material me as me, I'd carry around that burden to the exact extent I thought I was imperfect. The solution, my healing, came when I resorted to God, to my selfhood in Spirit as my only real identity—the Israel of me—and released my old, false beliefs about myself.

The world's solutions are available on every hand to every problem we face. Any one of us can go to a bookstore and come out with an armload of books filled with human advice on self-improvement. On not worrying. On health, on personal relations. On a wide variety of subjects. But doesn't this human advice usually deal mainly with the Jacob of us—trying to make him better, richer, healthier, and happier? Trying to make the materially imperfect over into something we can get along with?

Isn't our real course to resort to the source of all good? To God, Himself?! Not as an escape *from* reality, but as an establishment of all that is real—as a reclamation of our true identity.

A passage from the Bible puts it better than I can: "That ye put off concerning the former conversation the old man, which is corrupt according to the deceitful lusts; and be renewed in the spirit of your mind; and that ye put on the new man, which after God is created in righteousness and true holiness." [6]

Dreamlike Material Existence Can be Seen Through

How can we speed this renewing? Perhaps we can think of it as somewhat like waking from a dream. How many of you, for instance, have awakened from a dream—well, not quite awakened? Not in, but not quite out, either? Well, awakening from our material selfhood is a little like this in-between state of awareness. We're waking up in stages, a little at a time.

We can be aroused, say, from believing we fear to drive a car, yet still may feel we fear thunderstorms. In other words, we still have some waking up to do. But what we might call "the awake of us" is there—and felt. And as we apply that "awake" to a particular portion of the dream, that phase dissolves. And that higher sense of us replaces it. Instead of trying to patch up or change the dream of a material selfhood, what we're really doing is awakening to our perfect, spiritual selfhood in God. Putting off the old man (no matter how he tries to justify staying) and renewing what for all time has been true about us, the new man—the perfect expression of Spirit, God.

Just as Jesus through the power of God identified with the best there was of him—the Christ. Just as Jacob through the power of God was put off, and Israel emerged. Just as I, through the power of God, identified with the new man, I expressed my real identity more exactly. I saw God doesn't include inharmony; therefore, His expression, man, doesn't either.

So my old false sense of man was to be put off. And no matter how tightly it said it held me, it was dissolved like the bad dream it was. And I more fully expressed what was for all time true about me, in the exact proportion of my releasing the dream of me for that awake of me, my real nature.

An experience of somebody I know makes this awakening process clear. He was calling on a chief executive of a large manufacturing company. This company had exhausted its research abilities trying to solve the downward sales trend of one of its products. An improved competitive product was all but putting it out of business in one of its most productive sales areas.

My friend was tempted to sympathize with the tale of woe, but caught himself. He saw that if he steeped himself in the problem, he wasn't going to be in any position to correct it. He saw he couldn't go deeper into the dream if he hoped to wake up from it.

So right while the executive was describing the sad state of affairs, my friend aroused his thought to his real, unlimited, spiritual nature. Mentally, he related himself to God as his source, the source of all right thinking, therefore of all real solutions. As he did this, a new concept, something he had never envisioned before, began to take form in his thinking. From where? From the unlimited, spiritual intelligence called "God," the source of all good.

At first the concept was hazy. But, as Christian Scientists, both my friend and his business partner turned further and further to divine intelligence,

·their true selfhood in God. In short, they prayed. And step-by-step the new product idea developed and became clear. They finally constructed a prototype; and it was a solution. The company patented the product; and it proved helpful to their business and their volume.

Divine Spirit Provides the Impulsion to Awaken

Now, we can no more look to the material man or the material world for any real improvement or solution than we can look to the dream to find the awake of it. We can't find perfection in imperfection. That would be a little like looking to our thirst for refreshment.

This waking up process isn't as simple as turning off the alarm in the morning when we wake up from our night-dream. It's a continual elevation of our thought, more comparable to mountain climbing. Each minute, each day, each year we can progress until we reach the spiritual heights. It takes some work. It takes some discipline. But here's the important point: every step we take is impelled by God Himself, by divine Spirit working irresistibly within us.

In my own experience, my higher selfhood kept nudging me amid all that clamor and self-justification. A little push here, a tap there. And regardless of how dim the voice, I did hear it. Just a little, but enough to realize my healing. As long as

I related to a worldly me—as long as Jacob related to a worldly self as him—well, we'd both be going further and further in the wrong direction.

But as we resort to our source, or God, our spiritual nature expresses itself into our human experience. When I consistently began to identify with my higher spiritual selfhood, not only was my back healed but my whole life took on new forms of goodness—and this healing, this change, wasn't the result of human effort, of improved human thinking. I did make an effort and my human thinking did improve; but the power to achieve this came right from God, Himself. Under this enforcing spiritual goodness my employment developed and changed. I found myself doing much more creative things. And found more joy in everything I did. I found my relationships, business and home life more fulfilling.

Science and Health tells us, "God, Spirit, alone created all, and called it good. Therefore evil, being contrary to good, is unreal, and cannot be the product of God."[7]

God, Spirit, holds for us all the good there is. The continuing and loving demand He makes upon us is to relate to Him and to our spiritual selfhood—not to fall from the spiritual heights. Then we find our whole experience increasingly spiritual, more loving, and healthy through His power. We begin to know the presence of God in our daily life. Whether we're a homemaker, or teacher, or salesman, or a student, our need is to relate to God as our Mind, as our intelligence, to God as our Spirit, as our motivation, to God as impelling Love. Then we find whatever we're about lifted and healed. We begin to see all as stemming from God, ever present Spirit, the source of all true selfhood, the real of all of us.

Mary Baker Eddy Set an Example of One Who Wrestled Mightily

In her brief autobiography Mrs. Eddy writes of man's true origin: "War is waged between the evidences of Spirit and the evidences of the five physical senses; and this contest must go on until peace be declared by the final triumph of Spirit in immutable harmony." [8] And a little farther on she describes how this triumph must be won, "Divine Science demands mighty wrestlings with mortal beliefs, as we sail into the eternal haven over the unfathomable sea of possibilities." [9]

Mrs. Eddy wrote these words out of the depths of her own experience. It was through mighty wrestlings that she proved the power of right identification in her own life. She went through years of loneliness, ill health, and frustration.

Then one winter's evening, in 1866, she had an accident which looked like the end for her. Those around her held little hope for recovery. She was, in effect, placed squarely in the worldly self and pronounced by the worldly thought to be in critical condition.

Yet, this woman turned to her Bible and to the inspiration it contains. In a flash of profound inspiration, she glimpsed that God, divine Spirit, is absolutely all that really is. She began to see the "nothingness" of the worldly, material self. As she held to her understanding of her spiritual identity, this realization expressed itself more clearly in her human experience. Much to her friends' amazement, she was instantaneously freed. Like a dream her false sense of injury left her. She was healed.

For the next three years Mrs. Eddy continued to follow her spiritual, her highest nature. She wrote, and then in 1875 shared the results of her discovery in the book *Science and Health*.

During this progressive period she struggled with the world, but her struggle was a hopeful one. Mrs. Eddy was a devout woman. She'd loved and followed the church of her childhood. But the need to share her discovery impelled her to organize a church of her own.

As this went on, some of the clergymen of the day vigorously attacked her discovery. It's not hard to see why when we recognize the very basis of their faith as being challenged. Like them, she proclaimed the infinite nature of God. But unlike most of them, she saw man as Godlike, perfect. Nothing could dissuade her from her God-impelled expression of this revelation.

It's difficult for us to envision the trials of this woman as she stood up to the press and theologians of that day! You recall how you graciously applauded when I was introduced? Well, one time, according to newspaper accounts reported in a biography by Robert Peel, Mrs. Eddy was to give a talk to some two thousand. She came out, much I suspect as I did, was introduced and—icy stillness—no applause at all. Stony silence. But she gave a rousing, fearless address—and when it was over, except for a few pockets of supporters again icy, stony silence.

But she was undaunted. She must have felt her wholeness in God and persevered. Courage, bolstered by her love for mankind, moved her on. She didn't hesitate. She says of her years of intensive Bible research before writing *Science and Health*: "The search was sweet, calm, and buoyant with hope, not selfish nor depressing . . . The revelation of Truth in the understanding came to me gradually and apparently through divine power." [10] As more heard her message, more felt this same wonderful impulse of Love. And grateful thousands came and many were healed. As she identified in divine Love, she was impelled by Love in all she did. And her church has spread over the globe.

Putting God First Brings Transformation

We, each of us, can feel the impetus of divine Love in our lives as we put divine Love first in our lives. This impetus is the call of God Himself, to our consciousness, coming through the Christ, just as it was for Mrs. Eddy. And as we value our perfect selfhood, already intact in God, He reveals it to us. He reveals our lives as the expression of divine Life and Love as already complete, as spiritual, strong.

As complete ideas of Mind, God, we're intelligent. As complete ideas of divine Spirit, we're wholly spiritual. As the outcome of divine Love, we express the total fulfillment of Love.

We're not in bits and pieces, or parts. We're inseparable from the whole that's God, Himself.

Humanly, an idea comes in stages or parts. First, it's conceived or invented. Then it may—or may not—be activated. And, finally, though rarely, it's profitable or worthwhile. But with the over-view, the high-view of Christian Science, these steps or stages are but an incomplete recognition of the whole.

Let me illustrate what I mean with a book. As I turn this edge toward you, it's about all you can see. And as I put this end toward you, again, it's about all you can see. This one, the same. But, obviously, the book is whole and includes all of its parts all of the time. It's just our viewpoint we need to correct.

Just so in our view of everything that expresses God. It's never limited to fractional parts. It's complete, and we need to identify ourselves consistently with our true selfhood in God, Mind. We need to see the developing nature of this wholeness in our human lives.

Even though we may have been conditioned to accept fragmentation or limitation, we have innate power to reject anything that would obstruct our view of the completeness of God, good, and of man, His perfect expression.

We are complete. Every idea and activity of God is complete. And He has the responsibility of maintaining this completeness. He relates us to Himself, to our spiritual source. He brings the very best there is to our human experience. In truth there's no experience that isn't impelled by God. We hear a lot these days about establishing priorities. The priority of knowing life spiritually, of turning to God as the spiritual reality of all being—of seeing a whole new view of man and the universe as Divinity unfolding itself, of seeing from the spiritual heights—shouldn't this be our first priority? This will give us the courage and strength to wrestle with and overcome the old false sense of self whenever it tries to attach itself to us.

Rather than just talk about it, why not do something about it? Why not practice establishing your priority? The next time anger, irritation, embarrassment or something similar tempts you, establish your priority. Be grateful for your right to be your real Christly self and refuse to be anything else. Stop right in the middle of a sentence, or the act; let the momentum that tries to keep you going in the wrong direction continue, but without you. Just wave good-bye! It's your real selfhood rejecting the old outworn self. It's your spiritual selfhood exposing whatever would try to attach itself to you. You can dismiss it as not yours or anyone's.

Yes, there's no way of appreciating the merit of something like proving it works. And as we establish our priority of putting God first, of identifying in divine Love, we see the purity of Love expressed in our lives. And, regardless of how Jacob struggles, no matter how he wrestles—our real peace, the best of us, must eventually be expressed in the Israel of us.

Proving Our Real Selfhood is Worth the Struggle

A young lady I know came to a Christian Science practitioner's office. It was her first visit. A faint but real hope had brought her. Her situation was desperate and steadily getting worse: extreme nervousness, severe headaches, insomnia and depression.

She'd been seeing a psychiatrist regularly for over 6 years. The prescribed drugs she was taking to relieve anxiety and pain were having less and less effect as her tolerance to them grew. To get even a little relief she was now taking double the prescribed amounts every day. To get quiet enough to sleep or to get up for her job, she felt she needed to increase even that. The effects were severe—a gnawing, growing reliance on these drugs. Not only were her tensions and pain increasing, but she now had a growing addiction to the drugs.

As if this weren't enough, she was living with a man she wasn't married to. He drank heavily, often verbally abusing her. She didn't see anything morally wrong in living with him—only that it was uncomfortable at times.

In this first and in subsequent visits, she and the practitioner talked of who she really was. Increasingly she began to feel and live this spiritual selfhood. She learned to pray, also to affirm her real nature and to deny the false dreamlike self. Slowly at first, her reliance lifted from the drugs as she saw her spiritual completeness. Then, just four weeks from her first visit to the practitioner's office, she put aside the use of drugs.

Now every step this young lady took demanded new and higher views of her true selfhood, and a willingness to let go of who she thought she was. The insomnia and nervousness left. Soon the depression and headaches did too. As she continued to relate to her true selfhood in Love, she also saw the Jacob of her as limited, and often, indulgent. She recognized her freedom in being her true spiritual self, right from God. She found this freedom expressed in helping others, really helping them, never in indulging their appetites or selfishness.

The pure views of Love she was now identifying with led her to have the man she was living with move to an apartment of his own. Now this is important, not once had the practitioner indicated this step, nor any human step she took. Nor was this merely conforming to society's standards. She was living the very best she knew right out from God, pure Love. Her job, her friends, her family, all are the grateful beneficiaries of her new found physical and moral freedom. She had learned to put God, divine Love, first.

Such a priority changed Jacob's life. Such a priority changed the course of history in Jesus' life. It healed my body and changed my life. God, impartial Love, as the source of our identity! *Impartial* divine Love. Unlimited, divine presence. For instance, physically, as I stand here, I'm expressing partiality. I'm nearer physically to you than to you. Even if I moved over to where you are, I'd obviously then be nearer to you than to you.

Physicality by its very nature is partial, limited. It's always more here than there. But Love, divine consciousness, is boundless and ever present. It's here and there. It may be expressed in a location, but it's never confined by nor limited to that expression. Anymore than the idea of, say, worth or goodness is limited to or confined by someone in the next county doing something worthwhile. His doing good doesn't limit us from expressing good.

Good *is*. It's present in all directions. And Love is. And this oneness is present in all directions. One infinite Love represented infinitely. One Love . . . not two, twelve . . . or even 2 million loves, but one Love. Not only is God our Mind, the source of all intelligence, but God is our Love and the source of all our affection, our motivation and purpose.

As we relate to our true source in the one Love, this impelling goodness, this Spirit, expresses itself in our human experience as pure affection, right appreciation, fulfilling warmth.

Impartial, ever-present God, your Mind and mine, your Love and mine. As we relate to our true source in the one Love, each of us expresses this oneness as individual completeness right now, right from the wholeness that is God, all Love. With such a priority of putting divine Love first, we find prejudices melt. False opinions vanish. All dissolved in God's impartial love we express. And do you know what else begins to dissolve in that impartial, spiritual, divine Love? Every worldly frailty, every limitation as to our health. Our physical well-being reflects our new, our high priority, and the spiritual man we really are—our Christ manhood—is increasingly expressed.

Spirit, God, is perceived as real, universal, eternal now. Spirit's expression, man and the universe, are seen as perfect, at peace.

So establish your priorities. Identify with the one you really are—your Godlike selfhood. And the next time a problem tempts you, stop right in the middle of whatever it says it is. Let divine Mind, God, direct. Wave good-bye, dismiss the problem as never yours or man's. Let divine Love direct your next steps, next words. Right from our highest spiritual sense of right impelled by God, the one Love.

In a way this is the wrestling which Jacob did, and he triumphed and won the name of "Israel," the man who saw God face to face. He lost nothing, but gained everything.

You've nothing to lose. You can prove your perfect selfhood by starting right now. God is absolutely All and includes us in divine Being. He knows us as entirely spiritual and perfect. He brings forth our completeness.

So be the you, you are. Be the you God knows.

1. Genesis 32:24
2. Ephesians 6:12
3. Thomas Carlyle, "Sartor Resartus" book 1 , chapter 9
4. Science and Health, p. 288
5. Ibid., p. 468
6. Ephesians 4:22-24
7. Science and Health,.p. 339
8. Retrospection and Introspection, p. 56
9. Ibid. p.57
10. Science and Health, p.109

ACKNOWLEDGMENTS

Much gratitude is expressed to The First Church of Christ, Scientist in Boston, Massachusetts. As both John Wyndham and Glen Livezey were members of the Christian Science Board of Lectureship, this Church held the copyrights to these lectures. Some years ago, their Legal Department worked over a period of two years, to turn over these copyrights to the family.

* * * * * * * * * *

Appreciation is also given to Michael G. Kelly for use of his wonderful photos, including the cover, of the Grand Canyon in Arizona. These were taken during his many hiking treks across the famous gorge. The last photograph is of Mike himself.